"The mission: Decode the secret recipes for America's favorite junk foods. Equipment: Standard kitchen appliances. Goal: Leak the results to a ravenous public."

—*USA TODAY*

KITCHEN WIZARD TODD WILBUR IS AT IT AGAIN, CRACKING THE CODES TO MORE OF AMERICA'S BRAND-NAME FAVORITES, SUCH AS:

- A & W® ROOT BEER with the "frosty mug taste." No, you don't have to dig up any roots or buy any beer. All you need is a root beer concentrate found in most grocery stores ... and an unexpected secret ingredient.

- LITTLE CAESAR'S® CRAZY SAUCE®. Who would have dreamed that this great Italian sauce originated in Detroit! Now you can whip up a batch at home and have a great fresh pizza sauce or a dipping sauce to use with—what else!—LITTLE CAESAR'S® CRAZY BREAD®.

- NESTLÉ® CRUNCH®. This classic candy bar is incredibly easy to make ... especially since Nestlé conveniently provides you with its own incomparable chocolate right in the baking aisle of your supermarket.

"There's something almost magically compelling about the idea of making such foods at home.... The allure [of *Top Secret Recipes*] is undeniable, and it's stuffed with tidbits and lore that you're unlikely to find anywhere else."

—*BOSTON HERALD*

TODD WILBUR is the author of *Top Secret Recipes*. When not taste-testing recipes on himself, his friends, or TV talk-show hosts, Todd eats at the McDonald's® in his hometown of Emmaus, Pennsylvania.

TODD WILBUR

MORE

TOP SECRET

RECIPES

MORE FABULOUS KITCHEN
CLONES OF AMERICA'S
FAVORITE BRAND-NAME FOODS

WITH ILLUSTRATIONS BY THE AUTHOR

A PLUME BOOK

PLUME

Published by the Penguin Group
Penguin Books USA Inc., 375 Hudson Street, New York, New York 10014, U.S.A.
Penguin Books Ltd, 27 Wrights Lane, London W8 5TZ, England
Penguin Books Australia Ltd, Ringwood, Victoria, Australia
Penguin Books Canada Ltd, 10 Alcorn Avenue, Toronto, Ontario, Canada M4V 3B2
Penguin Books (N.Z.) Ltd, 182–190 Wairau Road, Auckland 10, New Zealand

Penguin Books Ltd, Registered Offices:
Harmondsworth, Middlesex, England

First published by Plume,
an imprint of Dutton Signet,
a division of Penguin Books USA Inc.

First Printing, November, 1994
9   10   8

REGISTERED TRADEMARK—MARCA REGISTRADA

LIBRARY OF CONGRESS CATALOGING IN PUBLICATION DATA:

Wilbur, Todd.
More top secret recipes : more fabulous kitchen clones of America's favorite brand-name foods / Todd Wilbur : with illustrations by the author.
p.   cm.
ISBN 0-452-27299-8
1. Cookery, American. 2. Junk food. I. Title.
TX715.W6584   1994
641.5973—dc20   94-14369
                                                      CIP

Printed in the United States of America
Set in Gill Sans Light and Machine

Designed by Steven N. Stathakis

To my doctor, Stanley Silverman,
for his comforting reassurance that
my cholesterol count has not yet
reached dangerously high levels.

ACKNOWLEDGMENTS

A book like this could not have been completed without the efforts of many. To these people, I cordially extend my thanks for their contributions, whether large or small.

At Plume, to Julia Moskin, Carole DeSanti, Tracey Guest, Lisa Johnson, Elaine Koster, and anyone else who put faith and hard work into this project, and who helped to make sense of my fragmented sentences and misplaced modifiers, and turn them into a book.

To my patient taste testers, critics and very close friends, who helped me with words of advice, and who slapped sense into me when I slipped into sugar shock: Ellen Geiger, Bob Stein, Ronnie Rubino, Allen Caminiti, Felipe Bascope, Scott Layer, JoEllen Kleckner, Beverly Reiley, Brother Scott, Dick and Jane, Velma, Tom and Sue Anthony, Maryland National Mortgage Company, spunky Deidre Strain, and Zebu the Wonder Chow.

Thank you all.

C O N T E N T S

A LITTLE FOREWORD

As with the first *Top Secret Recipes,* each of these recipes was subjected to an array of bakings and mixings, batch after batch, until the closest representation of the actual commercial product was finally achieved. I did not swipe, heist, bribe, or otherwise obtain any formulas through coercion or illegal means. I'd like to think that many of these recipes are the actual formulas for their counterparts, but there's no way of knowing for sure. In such cases of closely guarded secret recipes, the closer one gets to matching a real product's contents, the less likely it is that the protective manufacturer will say so.

The objective here is to match the taste and texture of our favorite products with everyday ingredients. In most cases, obtaining the exact ingredients for these mass-produced foods is nearly impossible. For the sake of security and convenience, many of the companies have contracted confidentially with vendors for the specialized production and packaging of each of their products' ingredients. These prepackaged mixes and ingredients are then sent directly to the company for final preparation.

Debbi Fields of Mrs. Fields Cookies, for example, arranged with several individual companies to custom manufacture many of her cookies' ingredients. Her vanilla alone is specially blended from a variety of beans grown in various places around the world. The other ingredients—the chocolate, the eggs, the sugars, the flour—all get specialized attention specifically for the Mrs. Fields company. The same holds true for McDonald's, Wendy's, KFC, and most of the big-volume companies.

Even if you could bypass all the security measures and somehow get your hands on the secret formulas, you'd have a hard time executing the recipes without locating many ingredients usually impossible to find at the corner market. Therefore, with taste in mind, substitution of ingredients other than those that may be used in the actual products is necessary to achieve a closely cloned end result. Happy cloning!

INTRODUCTION

When I started making kitchen clones, I wasn't sure how many people would be interested in squirting cream into a spongy homemade Twinkie, or if anybody but me would have the urge to manufacture a giant Reese's Peanut Butter Cup or the impulse to erect a double-decker hamburger that tastes exactly like the world-famous Big Mac. In times of economic uncertainties, and international dilemmas, the six ingredients in an Orange Julius seemed insignificant. Besides, the hottest-selling cookbooks on the market were low-fat, low-calorie, watch-what-you-eat-or-you-might-explode, 350-page volumes written by Dr. So-And-So of the Healthy Spleen Institute.

But while *The T-Factor Fat Gram Counter* rode the *New York Times* best-seller list for months and months, Burger King and Hostess and Hershey were still raking in record revenues. As *Eat More, Weigh Less* by Dr. Dean Ornish sold thousands of copies a week, Keebler was introducing a new line of shortbread cookies and McDonald's was unveiling the Monster Mac—a half-pound Big Mac with four all-beef patties, special sauce, lettuce, cheese, pickles, onions, and sesame-seed bun. Sure, I enjoy digging into a low-fat casserole, or a chicken salad with only eight grams of saturated fat. But after several days of dishes like these, I get a craving to sink my teeth into a juicy burger or a candy bar. Looks like I'm not alone.

I like to think that for my readers, *Top Secret Recipes* is an oasis of junk food in a desert of health.

The food represented in the book is the kind of food that America grew up on: everybody's favorites, with great little product histories—the most popular and craved foods in the world. And what fun is a craving if we can't sneak out and fulfill it? That's the best part. *Top Secret Recipes* is filled with fun food. Plus, if we're in control of the manufacturing process, we can customize our favorite brand-name foods to suit our tastes. We can put as much filling as we want to inside our Twinkies. And if our favorite part of Cracker Jack is the peanuts, we can add twice as many. We can have a burger that tastes like it was made by Carl's Jr., or a Butterscotch Krimpet that tastes like it was made by Tastykake, even if we don't live in the regions of the country where these goodies are available. And when we make these things at home, we save a little money and we know they're fresh.

As word about *Top Secret Recipes* spread, requests for more recipes came in. Somebody in Universal City, Texas, wanted to know how to make Oreo Cookies. Someone in Cedar Rapids, Iowa, wondered if it was possible to make a Milky Way at home. And a couple of guys in Costa Mesa, California, longed to know everything about Super Pretzels and whether it was possible to make Snapple Iced Tea. These were challenges I couldn't ignore. The seed was planted, it took root, and out popped *More Top Secret Recipes*.

Like the first one, this book is the result of some tedious spadework, some serious frustrations, and my denying myself the recommended daily allowance of fresh air. Once again, I've made every attempt to test the recipes thoroughly and come as close to the original product as store-bought ingredients allow. I've trashed my kitchen, scratched up my sink, and stained my countertops all in the name of copycat cooking. And it was all worth it.

THE QUESTIONS. THE ANSWERS.

After the first *Top Secret Recipes* came out, people had a lot of questions: "Why did you write this book?" "How did you write this book?" "Can I have a free book?" I started jotting the questions down in case I ever had an occasion to use them. This is that occasion. Here are several of the questions I've been asked most often along with their nearly spontaneous answers.

1. How did you learn to cook?

I started cooking when I was a kid, just because I was hyperactive and had to be doing something at all times. I made cookies. I cooked eggs. I made cookies in eggs. And, yes, I made a mess.

Eventually, I went off to college and was forced to learn a whole new culinary skill. The food in the dining halls was terrible, so those of us who wanted to eat something other than that prison food had to be resourceful. We were too broke to go out, so we designed a whole menu of cheap food that could be cooked in a toaster oven or hot pot. English muffin pizzas. Tuna melts. Top ramen. Kraft macaroni and cheese. Then we would invent new, creative dishes. Nacho popcorn (popcorn with sliced cheese melted over it.) Leftover pizza casserole (cut pizza slices into pan, add macaroni and cheese, bake). Ramen stew (top ramen mixed with bits of anything edible). These were staples of my college existence and my early culinary training.

Life after college was the real training ground. One of my many jobs was at a dinner theater called The Harlequin in Orange County, California. I was a waiter in the ritzy section of the theater, the balcony, where I had to learn to make Caesar salads at the table and flambé desserts without scorching any eyebrows. This is where my interest in gourmet cooking was piqued. And where, unfortunately, I was fired within a month for spending too much time backstage talking to the actresses.

But I kept cooking on my own, as anyone does out of the necessity to eat. It was in 1987 that I received in the mail the chain-letter recipe that was supposedly the "Secret Recipe" for Mrs. Fields Cookies. It wasn't actually the secret recipe, but it had become a very popular chain letter, one that had been distributed throughout the country by people who thought they had the real secret. I tried the recipe and the cookies were good, but I knew Mrs. Fields Cookies. I loved Mrs. Fields Cookies. These were *not* Mrs. Fields Cookies!

So I set out to improve the recipe. I went to the nearest Mrs. Fields outlet and got my hands on an ingredients list for her cookies, and went to work. Batch after batch, I experimented and eventually came up with a cookie that tasted like the real thing. I figured I'd see what else I could duplicate. How about a Big Mac? I went to McDonald's, bought the real thing, and took it apart. It wasn't hard to find a dressing like the "Special Sauce" (Kraft Thousand Island) and then to build a burger the same way McDonald's teaches it at Hamburger University.

I spent the next five years learning about cooking from the inside out. I cooked and baked and boiled to create clone recipes of famous foods. I learned the properties of different ingredients—which would thicken or sweeten, which would brown, when to fry. I learned from doing it over and over again, out of curiosity.

As I continued adding clone recipes to my growing list, I realized it would make a fun book. I did some line drawings of the products, put it all together, and eventually found a publisher who didn't think I was entirely nuts.

2. What have you heard from companies whose products you are copying?

Nothing. Not one of these companies has contacted me or my publisher to complain or otherwise comment about the book or any product that is represented.

I hope any company represented in a volume of *Top Secret Recipes* realizes that it is because its products are popular enough to warrant inclusion, and that imitation is the sincerest form of flattery.

3. How do you figure out the recipes for these products?

If it's a packaged product, I'll start with the ingredients list. Thanks to an FDA law, ingredients must be listed in descending order of their percentages in the product. Most of the main ingredients are easy to find at any supermarket. I just ignore the chemicals and preservatives that usually show up in small amounts at the end of the ingredients list, since we're going to eat the food fresh and don't have to worry about spoiling.

I then try to assemble the product in a test batch, which usually comes out tasting pretty horrible. From there it's just a matter of using more of some ingredients and less of others until the finished product tastes like the original. It may take only a couple of attempts to get it right, or it may take dozens.

Cooking times and preparation techniques can often be determined from recipes I've collected for products similar to the one I'm trying to clone. For example, if I want to make biscuits that taste like Popeye's Famous Biscuits, I may find a recipe for generic biscuits to give me a starting point and adjust it to match the brand-name original.

For products that don't have ingredients lists, like fast-food items, I use my own sense of taste. I take the product home and disassemble it, and then attempt to reassemble it with ingredients bought at a grocery store. Some products can't be duplicated because the basic ingredients aren't available. The BK Broiler at Burger King, for example, requires a specially processed slab of chicken that can't be found at most supermarkets. That's why it's not in this book.

Not only can the entire process be very time-consuming and frustrating, but it tends to get a bit expensive when I have to go through several versions of one recipe until I get it right. But I have to say, it's a thrill to finally come up with a recipe for a finished product that tastes exactly like the famous brand-name food.

4. Don't you have to do a lot of dishes?

Yes, I do. But I've learned that if you run really hot water at full blast over anything long enough it will eventually come clean.

5. What do you do with all that food you make?

Most of the rejects that don't come out like the original are still perfectly tasty. I give those to friends or neighbors, even my dog, just as I do most of the recipes that finally come out perfect. I like to get a little feedback from time to time to see if someone other than me thinks the recipe is a good one.

6. What was the hardest recipe to crack?

I would have to say that the hardest so far have been the Oreo Cookie and the Super Pretzel, both of which are in this book. I wanted to be sure the Oreo filling was just the right consistency. With a product as popular as Oreos, I realized that if it's not right, people are going to know. Just about everybody has eaten Oreos since they were kids, and they'll notice if it doesn't pass the test.

With the Super Pretzel, creating the right mixture of water and baking soda to dip each pretzel in before baking is extremely important. This is called a caustic bath, and is important in creating the chemical reaction with the dough that gives the finished product its shiny, golden brown appearance. This took some time because, hey, I'm no chemist.

Both recipes, I'm proud to say, came out great—and I know you'll think they taste just like the originals.

7. After testing all these recipes, aren't you a huge, fat pig?

I'm not huge, and I'm not fat. I'm 6' 1" and weigh 190 pounds. Although, yes, I am a pig.

8. When you're not working on one of these books, do you eat all this stuff anyway?

You bet. The books originated out of my true passion for "convenience food." And I know there are a lot of other people out there who get secret cravings for the items featured in my books, whether they'll admit it or not. America loves this food. It's all around us, and fast-food chains are still opening stores at a rate of nine or ten a week. Somebody's buying it.

Yes, I eat this stuff. But not all the time. I do think it's important to balance your diet with healthful, low-fat meals. I just eat this type of food when I get irresistible cravings. Like I did yesterday. And the day before that. And the day before that.

9. What if I make a recipe and it doesn't taste like the real thing?

Gosh, I don't know what to say. Maybe you made it wrong. Maybe you made a mistake. Maybe you scorched your taste buds on hot coffee one too many times and need expensive experimental microsurgery to restore those fragile sensors to their normal state. I'm just throwing out ideas here.

10. What criteria did you use for selecting the recipes to clone?

I know it seems like many of the *Top Secret Recipes* are for junk food or fast food (I like to call it "convenience food"), but that's only because I wanted to include recipes for the world's most popular products. And it just so happens that most of our beloved brand-name products fall into the junk-food or fast-food category.

As far as convenience food goes, many of the recipes here are reasonably health-conscious fare. I have included several recipes that are low in total fat and calories. Here's a sample of some of the recipes in this book with their fat counts:

RECIPE	FAT/GRAMS	CALORIES
Wendy's Grilled Chicken Fillet	9	320
Carl's Jr. Santa Fe Chicken	13	540
El Pollo Loco Chicken (3.5 ounces w/skin)	13	239
El Pollo Loco Chicken (breast w/skin)	7.6	193
Super Pretzel	0.5	175
Dunkin' Donuts Glazed Donut	9	200
Oreo Cookie (1)	2.1	49
Milky Way	3.9	118
3 Musketeers	4	140
A&W Root Beer	0	152

Keep in mind that you can use low-fat mayonnaise, dietetic sweeteners, and other substitutes, such as ground turkey instead of ground beef, in many of these recipes to accommodate your diet.

11. Why would people want to make these recipes at home if they can just as easily go out and buy the real thing?

This is a good question that I get asked all the time. And there are several possible answers.

1. *Cost.* It is actually less expensive to clone most of these products at home in your kitchen than it is to buy the originals.
2. *Taste.* Most of these goodies taste better fresh than they do after sitting on a store shelf for days, sometimes weeks.
3. *Availability.* Some of these brand-name products are only available in very limited regions of the country. Now you can enjoy anything in this book, anytime, anywhere.

4. *Customization.* Now you can cook your McDonald's hamburger the way *you* want to, or you can use dark chocolate on a candy bar that is only available with milk chocolate.
5. *Fun.* This is a cheap, fun, and harmless thrill.
6. *Curiosity.* You too can find out if it's really possible to make an Oreo at home. (It really is. Try it.)

12. How can I send you an idea for a recipe to crack?

I welcome any suggestions for recipes you may want to see in a future volume of *Top Secret Recipes*. Send your request to:

Todd Wilbur—Top Secret Recipes
c/o Plume Books
375 Hudson Street
New York, NY 10014–3657

SOME COOKING TIPS
FROM A GUY WHO CARES

Sometimes I can be a real idiot in the kitchen. I've wasted as many as four eggs when separating the whites by accidentally dropping in specks of yolk. I've often burned chocolate when melting it for dipping candy, and I've squandered hours on making dough for a simple recipe just because I forgot to look at the date on the package of yeast.

It was on these days that I determined there is a hard way to pick up little cooking hints, and there's an easy way. The hard way is by doing what I did—screwing up, then having to throw away your mistakes and run to the store in the pouring rain with a fistful of change to buy more ingredients so you can start the whole thing over again.

Then there is the easy way, which is to get cooking tips from somebody who learned the hard way.

SOME WORDS ABOUT CHOCOLATE

First off, some words about that delicate substance we call chocolate. Everybody's eaten it, but if you've cooked with it, you know it can be a pain—especially when the recipe requires that you melt it, as some of the recipes in this book do.

There are several different types of chocolate: sweet, semisweet, bittersweet, unsweetened, milk chocolate, and white chocolate (which actually isn't chocolate at all).

You will be using only semisweet and milk chocolate. Both are called for in the form of chocolate chips, which you buy by the bag. The most common are Nestlé and Hershey. Each company makes both milk chocolate and semisweet, and each works equally well.

I have found that the best place to melt chocolate is in the microwave. Semisweet chocolate is much easier to work with than milk chocolate, because it contains more chocolate liquor and no milk solids. Semisweet will melt to a much smoother, thinner consistency, and will not scorch as easily. This means that semisweet lends itself much more readily to dipping.

When melting either type of chocolate, use a microwave-safe glass or ceramic bowl that will retain heat. Set your microwave on half power and melt the chips for 1 minute. Stir. Rotate the bowl and microwave for another minute. Stir again. After 2 minutes, if the chocolate needs to melt more, heat it in 30-second intervals.

With milk chocolate, you have to find a delicate balance between microwaving and stirring. If you heat the chips too much, the chocolate will scorch. If you stir too much, the chocolate won't set up properly when you dip. Perfectly melted milk chocolate should set nearly as firm as it was in its original form at room temperature (68 to 70°F).

If you can't use a microwave to melt your chocolate, use a double boiler. You want to set the heat very low so that the water in the double boiler is only simmering and not boiling. Boiling water will scorch chocolate. Grease the inside of your double boiler lightly before you put the chocolate in and you'll be able to get practically all melted chocolate out of the pan.

For some of the recipes in this book, you may feel like substituting dark, semisweet chocolate instead of milk chocolate or even using white chocolate. It may be worth a try. How about a white-chocolate—covered Milky Way? Hmm.

And here's another tip to remember when making anything with chocolate. You can intensify the chocolate flavor by adding some vanilla to the recipe. You'll notice that this is what I've done with the recipes in the book for chocolate icings.

SOME WORDS ABOUT YEAST DOUGH

There are some recipes in this book that call for yeast dough, and I thought it was important to supply you with some pointers that will help you here and in the rest of your dough-making life.

The only yeast you'll need to use with this book is Fleischmann's—the type that comes in the three-envelope packages. That's the only kind I ever use. Always check to be sure the yeast you're using has not expired. Every package of yeast is stamped with an expiration date—usually eight to twelve months from the date you purchased it. Store your unopened yeast packages in the refrigerator.

When kneading dough, use your hands. This is much better than a wooden or plastic spoon because the warmth of your hands will help the yeast start rising (and it brings you back to those care-free Play-Doh days). When the dough pulls away from your hands easily, it has been kneaded enough.

One good way to get the dough rising is to put it in its bowl, uncovered, in the oven (the oven should be off) with a pan of boiling water. The hot water will start the dough rising right away, and the moisture from the water will keep the dough's surface from getting hard and dry.

You can tell when the dough has risen enough by sticking your finger into it up to the first knuckle. If the dough does not bounce back, it's ready. If it giggles, you're in a Pillsbury commercial.

SOME WORDS ABOUT SEPARATING EGGS

For the recipes that require egg whites, I've found that one of the easiest ways to separate the white from the yolk is to crack the egg with one hand into the other hand cupped over a small bowl. The egg whites will run out between your fingers, and you will be holding just the yolk in your hand. You can also use a small funnel. Just crack the egg into the funnel, and the egg white will run through, leaving the yolk. Use a container other than the bowl you will be beating the whites in. You don't want to risk ruining all the whites if some yolk should fall through.

If an accident should happen and you do get some yolk into the whites, use one of the egg shells to scoop out the yolk. Strangely, the shells act like a magnet for the specks of stray yolk.

To save your yolks for another recipe, slide them into a small bowl or cup, pour some cold water over them, and store them in the refrigerator. When you want to use the yolks, just pour off the water and slide the yolks into your recipe.

By the way, as a general rule in this book and any other cookbook, when a recipe calls for eggs and does not specify size, always use large eggs. Medium or extra-large eggs could throw off your measurements.

SOME WORDS ABOUT BAKING

Every once in a while, you should check your oven thermostat with an oven thermometer. I did and found out that my oven was off by twenty-five degrees. That's normal. It can be off by twenty-five degrees in either direction, but if it's any more than that, you should make adjustments when cooking, and get it fixed.

When baking, allow at least fifteen minutes for your oven to preheat. This is especially important if you do not have an indicator light that tells you when your oven is ready.

Several recipes in this book call for baking on cookie sheets. I highly recommend using two cookie sheets and alternating them, putting one sheet in the oven at a time. This will allow you to let one sheet cool before loading it up for the next run. If you don't let the sheet cool, your cooking time may be inaccurate because the dough will start to heat before you put the sheet into the oven.

If you absolutely must bake more than one cookie sheet at a time, you'll have to extend the cooking time. It will take the oven longer to reach the proper temperature with more dough to heat.

If you're baking cookies, you can very easily make them all uniform in size by rolling the dough into a tube with the diameter you need, then slicing it with a very sharp knife.

Keep in mind, especially with cookies, that baked goods will continue to cook for a while even after they've come out of the oven unless you remove them to a rack. The cookie sheet or baking pan will still be hot, and the sugar in the recipe will retain heat. This is why many people tend to overcook their cookies. I know the feeling. When you follow suggested cooking times, it sometimes seems as though the cookies aren't done when they come out of the oven—and they probably aren't. But they'll be fine after sitting for some time on the cookie sheet.

SOME WORDS ABOUT HAMBURGER PATTIES

Just about every backyard hamburger cookout I've attended included hamburger patties that tipped the scale in size and weight. Most homemade burgers are way too thick to cook properly, and the added thickness doesn't add anything to the taste of the sandwich. In fact, if we cut the amount of beef we use in the hamburger patties, we're cutting out excess fat and calories, decreasing the chance that the burgers may not cook thoroughly, while not compromising anything in overall taste. At the same time, thicker patties tend to shrink up as they cook into unmanageable mutant forms, bulging in the middle, and stacking poorly onto buns and lettuce.

You'll notice that every hamburger recipe in this book requires a very thin patty. This is the way the experts in the business do it—the Dave Thomases, the Carl Karchers, the McDonald Brothers—for concerns over cost, taste and a thorough, bacteria-free cooking process. But just how do we get our patties so thin like the big boys, and still make them easy to cook without breaking? We freeze 'em, folks.

Plan ahead. Hours, even days, before you expect to make your hamburgers, pat the patties out onto wax paper on a cookie sheet with a diameter slightly larger than the buns you are using, and about $1/8$ to $1/4$ inch thick (with consistent thickness from center to edge). Thickness depends on the burger. If you're making a small hamburger, like the one at McDonald's, which is only about $1/8$ ounce before cooking, make the patties $1/8$ inch thick. If you're going for the Quarter Pounder, make your patty $1/4$ inch thick—never more than that. Lay wax paper over the top of your patties and put them in the freezer.

When your patties are completely frozen, it's time to cook. You can cook them straight out of the freezer on a hot grill or frying pan for 3 to 7 minutes per side, without worrying about thorough cooking. And the patties will flip easily without falling apart.

A&W
ROOT BEER

☆ ♥ ☎ ✎ ✈ ✉ ✂ ☞ ✿

On a hot summer afternoon in 1919, Roy Allen came up with a plan. He set up a roadside stand to sell cool drinks to spectators of a Veterans Day Parade in Lodi, California. For a nickel, thirsty parade-goers could knock back a tall glass of what would eventually become America's favorite root beer. The success of Allen's unique blend of roots, herbs, and berries led to three root beer concessions in Sacramento, California, all featuring carhop service—the first of the drive-in fast-food chains. Allen expanded his business further in 1922 when he formed a partnership with entrepreneur Frank Wright. This led to the name that would become famous, A&W, the country's best-selling root beer. In 1993 Cadbury Schweppes PLC, a British candy and beverage company, bought A&W Brands, Inc., for $334 million.

The root beer you'll make here is a simplified version of Roy Allen's method from the early 1900s. Instead of harvesting roots, herbs, and berries, you have the luxury of using a root beer concentrate that can be found in most grocery stores.

$3/4$ cup granulated sugar
$3/4$ cup hot water
1 liter cold seltzer water

$1/2$ teaspoon plus $1/8$ teaspoon root beer concentrate (McCormick is best)

1. Dissolve the sugar in the hot water.
2. Add the root beer concentrate and let cool.
3. Combine the root beer mixture with the cold seltzer water, drink immediately, or store in refrigerator in tightly covered container.
  • MAKES 5 CUPS

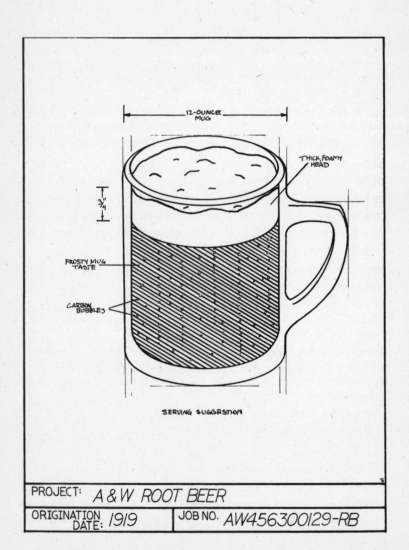

12-OUNCE MUG

THICK, FOAMY HEAD

3/4"

FROSTY MUG TASTE

CARBON BUBBLES

SERVING SUGGESTION

PROJECT:	A & W ROOT BEER
ORIGINATION DATE: 1919	JOB NO. AW456300129-RB

ARBY'S SAUCE

☆ ♥ ☎ ✎ ✈ ✉ ✂ ☛ ✿

In 1964, when the Arby's concept was created by brothers Leroy and Forrest Raffel, the name was supposed to be R.B., for Raffel Brothers, but that was expanded to the more familiar Arby's. Having marked its 30th year in 1994, Arby's is celebrating more than $1.5 billion in sales from 2,603 outlets. Arby's Miami headquarters took a bit hit in 1992 from Hurricane Andrew, the most damaging hurricane to hit Florida in decades, but the company bounced back and continued growing.

The company's unique sliced beef sandwiches offer customers a departure from hamburgers made of ground beef. This special barbecue sauce enhances a roast beef sandwich, as well as many other homemade and store-bought creations.

1 cup catsup	1/4 teaspoon pepper
2 teaspoons water	1/4 teaspoon salt
1/4 teaspoon garlic powder	1/2 teaspoon hot pepper sauce
1/4 teaspoon onion powder	(Tabasco is best)

1. Combine all the ingredients in a small saucepan and cook over medium heat, stirring constantly, until the sauce begins to boil, 5 to 10 minutes.
2. Remove the sauce from the heat. Cover and allow to cool.
3. Pour into a covered container for storage in your refrigerator. Keeps for a month or two.
- MAKES 1 CUP

. . . .

BAILEY'S ORIGINAL IRISH CREAM

☆ ♥ ☎ ✏ ✈ ✉ ✂ ☛ ✿

Bailey's launched its Irish Cream Liqueur in 1974, after years of development. The cream liqueur is based on an old Irish recipe using all-natural ingredients, including cream that is produced just for the Bailey's company. In fact, because the product line has become so successful, Bailey's accounts for one-third of Ireland's entire milk production. More than 4,000 farmers supply the 40 million gallons of milk used annually in producing cream for the liqueur. Bailey's now ranks number one among all liqueur brands in the world.

I cup light cream (<u>not</u> heavy cream)
One 14-ounce can Eagle sweetened
   condensed milk
1 ²/₃ cups Irish whiskey
1 teaspoon instant coffee

2 tablespoons Hershey's chocolate
   syrup
1 teaspoon vanilla extract
1 teaspoon almond extract

1. Combine all the ingredients in a blender set on high speed for 30 seconds.
2. Bottle in a tightly sealed container and refrigerate. The liqueur will keep for at least 2 months if kept cool. Be sure to shake the bottle well before serving.
- MAKES 4 CUPS

TIDBITS

If you can't find light cream, use half-and-half or whole milk (rather than heavy cream, which will tend to separate).

• • • •

CARL'S JR.
CHICKEN CLUB

☆　♥　☎　✎　✈　✉　✄　☛　✿

The first day's receipts at Carl Karcher's just-purchased hot-dog cart in 1941 totaled $14.75. Peanuts, right? But Karcher was determined to make it big. So during the next two years he purchased several more stands throughout the Los Angeles area, later expanding into restaurants and diversifying the menu. In 1993, what had once been a business of one tiny hot-dog cart had become a multi-million-dollar company with 642 outlets. From $14.75 on the first day to today's $1.6 million in daily receipts, old Carl was on the right track.

2 whole chicken breasts, skinned, boned, and halved
1 cup teriyaki marinade (Lawry's is best)
4 whole-wheat hamburger buns
8 slices bacon

1/4 cup mayonnaise
1 cup alfalfa sprouts, loosely packed
4 lettuce leaves
4 large tomato slices
4 slices Kraft Swiss Cheese Singles

1. Marinate the chicken in the teriyaki marinade in a shallow bowl for 30 minutes.
2. Preheat a clean barbecue to medium grilling heat.
3. Brown the faces of each bun in a frying pan on the stove. Keep the pan hot.
4. Cook the bacon in the pan until crisp, then set aside.
5. Grill the chicken breasts 5 to 8 minutes per side, or until cooked through.
6. Spread about 1/2 tablespoon of mayonnaise on the face of each bun, top and bottom.
7. Divide the sprouts into 4 portions and mound on each bottom bun.

8. On the sprouts, stack a lettuce leaf, then a slice of tomato.
9. Place one chicken breast half on each of the sandwiches, atop the tomato.

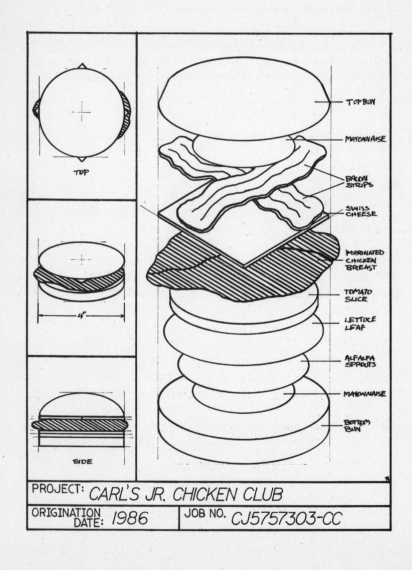

TOP

SIDE

TOP BUN

MAYONNAISE

BACON STRIPS

SWISS CHEESE

MARINATED CHICKEN BREAST

TOMATO SLICE

LETTUCE LEAF

ALFALFA SPROUTS

MAYONNAISE

BOTTOM BUN

4"

PROJECT: CARL'S JR. CHICKEN CLUB

ORIGINATION DATE: 1986

JOB NO. CJ5757303-CC

10. Next, stack a slice of Swiss cheese on the chicken, and then the 2 pieces of bacon, crossed over each other.
11. Top off the sandwich with the top bun.
12. Microwave for 15 seconds on high.

- MAKES 4 SANDWICHES

. . . .

CARL'S JR.
SANTA FE
CHICKEN

☆ ♥ ☎ ✎ ✈ ✉ ✄ ☞ ✿

This has to be one of my favorite fast-food sandwiches of all time. It's only been around since March of 1991, but has become a favorite for those familiar with Carl's Jr. outlets dotting the western United States. Today Carl's Jr. outlets can be found in California, Arizona, Utah, Nevada, Oregon, Mexico, Malaysia, China, Japan, and the Mideast. For all of you who live elsewhere, this is the only way you're going to get to try this fast-food treat. And it is worth trying.

2 whole chicken breasts, skinned, boned, and halved
1 cup teriyaki marinade (Lawry's is best)
$1/4$ cup mayonnaise
$1/4$ teaspoon paprika
$1/4$ teaspoon cayenne pepper

$1/4$ teaspoon curry powder
Pinch salt
4 whole-wheat hamburger buns
4 lettuce leaves
One 4-ounce can mild green chili peppers, well drained
4 slices American cheese

1. Marinate the chicken in the teriyaki marinade in a shallow bowl for 30 minutes.
2. Preheat a clean barbecue to medium grilling heat.
3. Prepare the sauce in a small bowl by mixing the mayonnaise with the paprika, cayenne pepper, curry powder, and salt.
4. Grill the chicken for 5 to 8 minutes per side, or until done.
5. Brown the faces of each bun in a hot frying pan.
6. Spread a tablespoon of sauce on the faces of each bun, top and bottom.
7. On each bottom bun place a lettuce leaf, then a green chili pep-

per. You want the pepper to be spread over most of the lettuce. To do this, slice the pepper down the middle and spread it open so that it covers more territory. When sliced open like this, some peppers are big enough for 2 sandwiches. Some are much smaller and enough for only one sandwich.

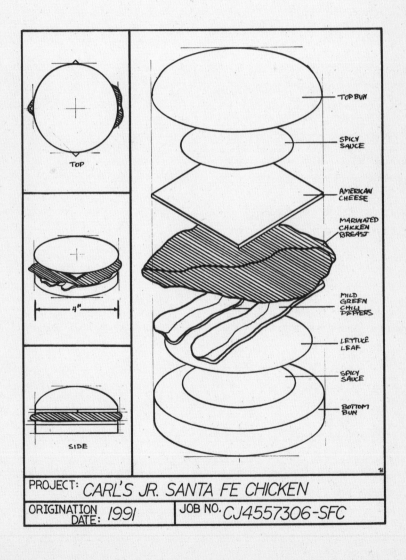

TOP

SIDE

TOP BUN

SPICY SAUCE

AMERICAN CHEESE

MARINATED CHICKEN BREAST

MILD GREEN CHILI PEPPERS

LETTUCE LEAF

SPICY SAUCE

BOTTOM BUN

PROJECT: CARL'S JR. SANTA FE CHICKEN

ORIGINATION DATE: 1991   JOB NO. CJ4557306-SFC

8. Place one chicken breast half on each of the sandwiches, on top of the chili pepper.
9. Place a slice of American cheese on the chicken.
10. Top it all off with the top bun.

· MAKES 4 SANDWICHES

· · · ·

CARL'S JR. WESTERN BACON CHEESEBURGER

☆   ♥   ☎   ✎   ✈   ✉   ✂   ☛   ✿

In 1989, Carl's Jr. became the first fast-food chain to allow customers to use their ATM cards to make purchases. Not only can customers buy a Western Bacon Cheeseburger and fries to go without using cash, they can get up to forty bucks out of their account.

The Western Bacon Cheeseburger is definitely up there on my list of favorite burgers. Onion rings, bacon, and cheese combine to make a tasty gut-grinder that can be thoroughly enjoyed when you're taking time off from the saturated-fat watch. The sandwich was introduced in 1983, and has since become so successful that it has spawned variations, from a junior version to the monstrous double, both of which are included here.

2 frozen onion rings
¹/₄ pound ground beef
1 sesame-seed hamburger bun
2 slices bacon
Salt to taste
1 slice American cheese

2 tablespoons Bull's-Eye Hickory Smoke barbecue sauce (you must use this brand and variety to make it taste just like Carl's; other brands will produce different, but still tasty, results)

1. Preheat a clean barbecue to medium grilling heat.
2. Bake the onion rings in the oven according to the directions on the package.
3. Form the ground beef into a flat burger the same diameter as the

bun. It's best to premake your burger and store it in the freezer, then cook it frozen.

4. Grill the faces of the top and bottom bun in a frying pan on the stove over medium heat. Keep the pan hot.

5. Cook the bacon slices in the pan.

6. Grill the burger for 3 to 4 minutes per side, or until done. Salt each side.

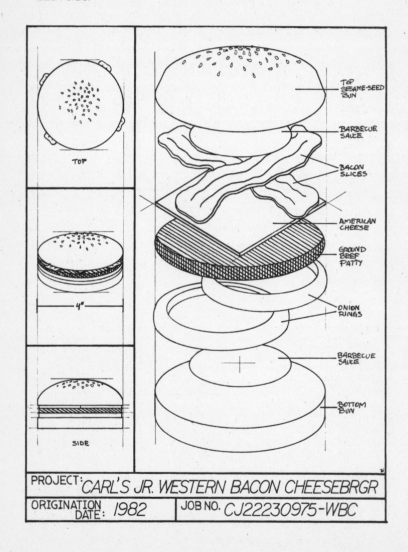

TOP

4"

SIDE

TOP SESAME-SEED BUN

BARBECUE SAUCE

BACON SLICES

AMERICAN CHEESE

GROUND BEEF PATTY

ONION RINGS

BARBECUE SAUCE

BOTTOM BUN

PROJECT: CARL'S JR. WESTERN BACON CHEESEBRGR

ORIGINATION DATE: 1982

JOB NO. CJ22230975-WBC

7. Spread 1 tablespoon of the barbecue sauce on the faces of each bun, top and bottom.
8. Place both onion rings on the sauce on the bottom bun. Next stack the burger, then the cheese and the 2 bacon slices, crossed over each other.
9. Top off the sandwich with the top bun.
- MAKES 1 SANDWICH

. . . .

Carl's Jr. Junior Western Bacon Cheeseburger®

For about a buck, Carl's Jr. sells this smaller version of the preceding sandwich. It's made with a slightly smaller bun, a smaller portion of beef, half the bacon, and half the onion rings.

Here's what you do: Pat out $1/8$ pound of ground beef to the same diameter as the bun. Use only one slice of bacon, broken in two, with the pieces crossed over each other. Use only one big onion ring, and build the burger in the same stacking order as the larger, original version.

Carl's Jr. Double Western Bacon Cheeseburger®

For real cholesterol fans, Carl's Jr. has designed a supersize version of this very popular burger. It is essentially the same as the original, with an additional $1/4$-pound patty of beef and an additional slice of American cheese stacked on top of the other cheese and beef. Everything else is made the same as in the original. If you try it you'll like it. Just remember to jog an extra mile.

TIDBITS

As I was experimenting, I discovered a variation of this sandwich that I think is pretty darn good. I called it a Western Bacon Chicken Sandwich, and it goes something like this:

Prepare your chicken by marinating and cooking it the same

way as in the Carl's Jr. Chicken Club or Santa Fe Chicken recipe. Then stack the sandwich as you would for a Western Bacon Cheeseburger, but using the chicken instead. Tastes great, less filling.

Carl, are you paying attention?

CINNABON CINNAMON ROLLS

☆　❤　☎　✎　✈　✉　✂　☞　❀

In early 1985, restaurateur Rich Komen decided there was a specialty niche in convenience-food service just waiting to be filled. His idea was to create an efficient outlet that could serve freshly made cinnamon rolls in shopping malls throughout the country. It took nine months for Komen and his staff to develop a cinnamon roll he knew customers would consider the "freshest, gooiest, and most mouthwatering cinnamon roll ever tasted." The concept was tested for the first time in Seattle's Sea-Tac mall later that year, with workers mixing, proofing, rolling, and baking the rolls in full view of the customers. Now, more than 200 outlets later, Cinnabon has become the fastest-growing cinnamon roll bakery in the country.

ROLLS

1 1/4-ounce package active dry yeast
1 cup warm milk (105 to 110°F)
1/2 cup granulated sugar
1/3 cup margarine, melted

1 teaspoon salt
2 eggs
4 cups all-purpose flour

FILLING

1 cup packed brown sugar
2 1/2 tablespoons cinnamon

1/3 cup margarine, softened

ICING

8 tablespoons (1 stick)
　　margarine, softened
1 1/2 cups powdered sugar

1/4 cup (2 ounces) cream cheese
1/2 teaspoon vanilla extract
1/8 teaspoon salt

1. For the rolls, dissolve the yeast in the warm milk in a large bowl.
2. Mix together the sugar, margarine, salt, and eggs. Add flour, and mix well.

3. Knead the dough into a large ball, using your hands dusted lightly with flour. Put in a bowl, cover, and let rise in a warm place about I hour, or until the dough has doubled in size.
4. Roll the dough out on a lightly floured surface. Roll the dough flat until it is approximately 21 inches long and 16 inches wide. It should be about ¼ inch thick.

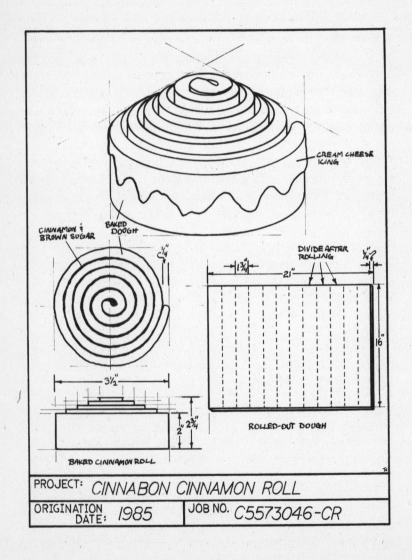

CREAM CHEESE ICING

CINNAMON & BROWN SUGAR

BAKED DOUGH

¼"

DIVIDE AFTER ROLLING

¼"?

1¾"

21"

16"

3½"

2" 2¾"

ROLLED-OUT DOUGH

BAKED CINNAMON ROLL

PROJECT: CINNABON CINNAMON ROLL

ORIGINATION DATE: 1985

JOB NO. C5573046-CR

5. Preheat oven to 400°F.
6. For the filling, combine the brown sugar and cinnamon in a bowl. Spread the softened margarine evenly over the surface of the dough, and then sprinkle the cinnamon and sugar evenly over the surface.
7. Working carefully from the top (a 21-inch side), roll the dough down to the bottom edge.
8. Cut the rolled dough into 1¾-inch slices and place 6 at a time, evenly spaced, in a lightly greased baking pan. Let the rolls rise again until double in size (about 30 minutes). Bake for 10 minutes, or until light brown on top.
9. While the rolls bake, combine the icing ingredients. Beat well with an electric mixer until fluffy.
10. When the rolls come out of the oven, coat each generously with icing.
- MAKES 12 ROLLS

TIDBITS

These rolls can be frozen after baking. Just pop one into the microwave for 20–30 seconds to reheat.

• • • •

DUNKIN' DONUTS

☆ ♥ ☎ ✎ ✈ ✉ ✂ ☛ ❀

As he worked long, hard days at a shipyard in Hingham, Massachusetts, during World War II, William Rosenberg was struck with an idea for a new kind of food service. As soon as the war ended, Rosenberg started Industrial Luncheon Services, a company that delivered fresh meals and snacks to factory workers. When Rosenberg realized that most of his business was in coffee and donuts, he quit offering his original service. He found an old awning store and converted it into a coffee-and-donut shop called The Open Kettle. This name was soon changed to the more familiar Dunkin' Donuts, and between 1950 and 1955 five more shops opened and thrived. The company later spread beyond the Boston area and has become the largest coffee-and-donut chain in the world.

Today, Dunkin' Donuts offers fifty-two varieties of donuts in each shop, but the most popular have always been the plain glazed and chocolate-glazed yeast donuts.

DONUTS

One ¼-ounce package active dry
    yeast
2 tablespoons warm water (98°F)
¾ cup warm milk (30 seconds in the
    microwave does the trick)
2½ tablespoons margarine or butter

1 egg
⅓ cup granulated sugar
1 teaspoon salt
2¾ cups all-purpose flour
3 cups vegetable oil

GLAZE

5⅓ tablespoons (⅓ cup)
    margarine or butter
2 cups powdered sugar

½ teaspoon vanilla extract
⅓ cup hot water

FOR CHOCOLATE GLAZE
1 cup semisweet chocolate chips

1. In a medium bowl, dissolve the yeast in the warm water.
2. Add the milk, margarine or butter, egg, sugar, and salt, and blend with an electric mixer until smooth.
3. Add half the flour and mix for 30 seconds.

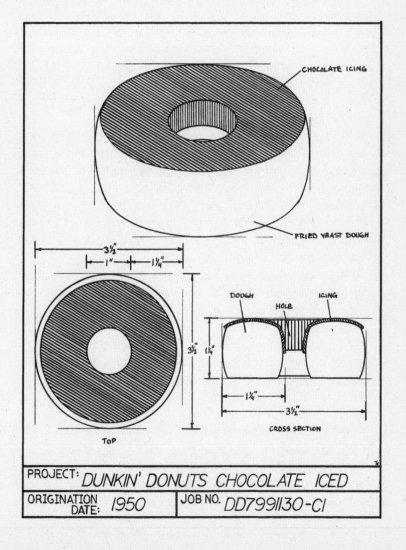

CHOCOLATE ICING

FRIED YEAST DOUGH

3½"
1"
1¼"
3½"
1¼"

TOP

DOUGH
HOLE
ICING

1¼"
3½"

CROSS SECTION

PROJECT: *DUNKIN' DONUTS CHOCOLATE ICED*

ORIGINATION DATE: *1950*

JOB NO. *DD7991130-C1*

4. Add the remaining flour and knead the dough with flour-dusted hands until smooth.

5. Cover the bowl of dough and leave it in a comfy, warm place until the dough doubles in size, about 1 hour. You can tell that the dough has risen enough when you poke it with your finger and the indentation stays.

6. Roll out the dough on a heavily floured surface until it's about $1/2$ inch thick.

7. If you don't have a donut cutter, and don't intend to buy one, here's a way to punch out your dough: Empty a standard 15-ounce can of whatever you can find—vegetables, refried beans, even dog food. Be sure to wash out the can very well, and punch a hole in the opposite end so that the dough won't be held inside the can by a vacuum.

8. When you've punched out all the dough (you should have about a dozen unholed donuts), it's time for the holes. Find the cap to a bottle of lemon juice or Worcestershire sauce, or any other small cap with a diameter of about $1 1/4$ inches. Use this to punch out holes in the center of each of your donuts.

9. Place the donuts on plates or cookie sheets, cover, and let stand in the same warm, comfy place until they nearly double in size. This will take 30 to 45 minutes.

10. Heat the vegetable oil in a large frying pan over medium heat. Bring the oil to about 350°F. It is easily tested with scrap dough left over from punching out the donuts. The dough should bubble rapidly.

11. Fry each donut for about 30 seconds per side, or until light golden brown. Cool 5 minutes on paper towels.

12. For either the plain or the chocolate glaze, combine the margarine or butter with the powdered sugar in a medium bowl and blend with an electric mixer.

13. Add the vanilla and hot water. Mix until smooth.

14. If you're making the chocolate glaze, melt the chocolate chips in a microwave-safe bowl in the microwave for 30 to 40 seconds. Stir, then microwave another 30 seconds and stir again until completely melted. Add to the plain glaze mixture. Blend until smooth.

15. When the donuts have cooled, dip each top surface into the glaze and then flip over and cool on a plate until the glaze firms up, about 15 minutes.

• MAKES 1 DOZEN DONUTS

• • • •

TIDBITS

You can also make "donut holes" as they do at Dunkin' Donuts by cooking and glazing the holes you've punched out the same way you prepared the donuts.

EL POLLO LOCO FLAME-BROILED CHICKEN

☆　♥　☎　✎　✈　✉　✂　☞　✿

Okay, time to brush up on your Spanish.

El Pollo Loco, or "The Crazy Chicken," has been growing like mad since it crossed over the border into the United States from Mexico. Francisco Ochoa unknowingly started a food phenomenon *internacional* in 1975 when he took a family recipe for chicken marinade and opened a small roadside *restaurante* in Gusave, Mexico. He soon had 90 stores in 20 cities throughout Mexico. The first El Pollo Loco in the United States opened in Los Angeles in December of 1980 and was an immediate success. It was only three years later that Ochoa got the attention of bigwigs at Denny's, Inc., who offered him $11.3 million for his U.S. operations. Ochoa took the deal, and El Pollo Loco grew from 17 to more than 200 outlets over the following decade. *¡Muy bien!*

2 cups water
4 teaspoons salt
2 teaspoons pepper
1 garlic clove

1 teaspoon yellow food coloring (or
　　a pinch of ground saffron)
2 tablespoons pineapple juice
1 teaspoon lime juice
1 whole frying chicken with skin,
　　halved or quartered

1. In a blender, combine the water, salt, pepper, garlic, and food coloring (or saffron). Blend on high speed for 15 seconds. Add pineapple juice and lime juice to marinade blend for 5 seconds.
2. Marinate the chicken in the liquid in a bowl or pan for 45 minutes. Turn and marinate for 30 minutes more.
3. Preheat a clean barbecue to medium-low grilling heat.

4. Cook the chicken on the open grill for 45 minutes to 1 hour, or until the skin is golden brown and crispy. Be sure the flames are not scorching the chicken, or the skin may turn black before the center is done. Lower the heat if necessary. (If you do not have a gas grill, you can spray a little water on the charcoal to keep the flames at bay.) Turn the chicken often as it cooks.
5. Cut the chicken into 8 pieces, with a large, sharp knife, cutting the breast in half and cutting the thighs from the legs.

• MAKES 8 PIECES

• • • •

EL POLLO LOCO
SALSA

☆　♥　☎　✎　✈　✉　✂　☞　✿

El Pollo Loco's success is based on its unique approach to fast food. The marinated, flame-broiled chicken is served with flour or corn tortillas and a fresh tomato salsa, so that hungry customers can strip the chicken from the bones and make their own soft tacos, smothered in spicy salsa. It's actually a very low-fat, low-calorie version of the fried chicken you normally find at a fast-food chain.

Use this salsa with the marinated chicken from the previous recipe wrapped in tortillas, or with other dishes.

2 medium tomatoes
1 fresh jalapeño pepper, stemmed,
　　or 10 slices canned jalapeños,
　　or "Nacho Slices"

$1/2$ teaspoon salt

1. Chop the tomatoes and jalapeños together until they have the consistency of a coarse puree. You can use a food processor, but stop chopping when the mixture is still quite coarse. There will be a lot of liquid, which you want to use as well. Pour everything into a medium bowl.
2. Add the salt to the mixture and stir.
3. Pour the salsa into a covered container and let it sit for several hours to allow the flavor to develop. Overnight is best.
- MAKES ABOUT 2 CUPS

• • • •

KEEBLER
PECAN SANDIES

☆　♥　☎　✎　✈　⊠　✂　☞　✿

This company was founded as the United Biscuit Company of America back in 1927. It was made up of sixteen bakeries from Philadelphia to Salt Lake City, marketing cookies and crackers under a variety of brand names. That system lasted for twenty-two years, and eventually the name Keebler was adopted for the entire conglomerate. Keebler was linked with the United Biscuit name once again after it was bought in 1974 by a British company of that name.

Today the company makes 50 billion cookies and crackers each year; among them are the popular Pecan Sandies, first sold in 1955. The Toffee variety came thirty-eight years later.

1 1/2 cups vegetable shortening	4 cups all-purpose flour
3/4 cup granulated sugar	1/4 teaspoon baking soda
1 1/2 teaspoons salt	2 tablespoons water
2 eggs	1 cup shelled pecans

1. Preheat the oven to 325°F.
2. In a large bowl, cream together the shortening, sugar, and salt with an electric mixer on medium speed.
3. Add the eggs and beat well.
4. While mixing, slowly add the flour, baking soda, and water.
5. Chop the pecans into very small bits using a food processor or blender on low speed. Be careful not to overchop; you don't want to make pecan dust. The pieces should be about the size of rice grains.
6. Add the pecans to the dough and knead with your hands until the pecans are well blended into the mixture.
7. Roll the dough into 1-inch balls and press flat with your hands

onto ungreased baking sheets. The cookies should be about 2 inches in diameter and ½ inch thick.

8. Bake for 25 to 30 minutes, or until the edges of the cookies are golden brown.

- MAKES 4 DOZEN COOKIES.

. . . . .

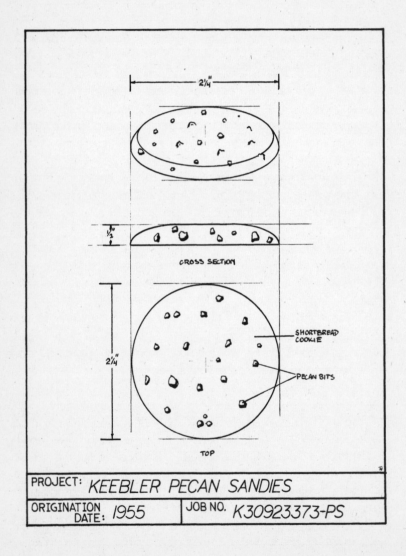

2¼"

½"

CROSS SECTION

2¼"

SHORTBREAD COOKIE

PECAN BITS

TOP

PROJECT: *KEEBLER PECAN SANDIES*

ORIGINATION DATE: *1955*   JOB NO. *K30923373-PS*

Keebler® Toffee Sandies®

Follow the Pecan Sandies recipe, above, replacing the chopped pecans with one 6-ounce package of Heath® Bits 'o Brickle®.

LITTLE CAESAR'S CRAZY BREAD

☆ ♥ ☎ ✎ ✈ ✉ ✂ ☛ ✿

In 1959, Michael Ilitch and his wife, Marian, opened the first Little Caesar's restaurant in Garden City, Michigan, fifteen miles west of Detroit. Encouraged by their success, the couple opened a second restaurant two years later, and soon Little Caesar's Pizza was a household name in the Detroit area. Biographical material provided by the company claims that Ilitch "thinks pizza," and that when he designed the Little Caesar's conveyer oven, the company was able to serve hot pizza faster than anyone else in the industry.

One of the most popular products available from Little Caesar's is the Crazy Bread, first served in 1982. It's just a pizza crust cut into eight pieces, then coated with garlic salt, butter, and Parmesan cheese.

One 10-ounce tube Pillsbury pizza
    dough
2 tablespoons (¼ stick) butter

1 teaspoon garlic salt
Kraft 100% grated parmesan
    cheese for topping

1. Preheat the oven to 425°F.
2. Unroll the dough on a cutting board. Position it lengthwise (longer from left to right than from top to bottom). With a sharp knife, cut the dough in half down the middle. Then cut each of those halves vertically in half, and then in half once more so that you have 8 even strips of dough.
3. Being careful not to stretch the dough, place each strip on a lightly greased cookie sheet and bake for 6 to 8 minutes, or until the top just turns golden brown.
4. While the dough bakes, melt the butter (on the stove or in the microwave on high for 15 to 20 seconds), then add the garlic salt and stir until it dissolves.

5. Remove the browned dough from the oven and with a pastry brush or spoon spread a coating of garlic butter over each piece.
6. Sprinkle a generous amount of Parmesan cheese on each.
- MAKES 8 PIECES

. . . .

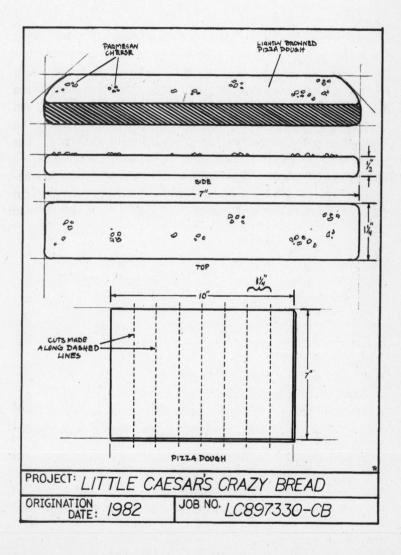

PARMESAN CHEESE

LIGHTLY BROWNED PIZZA DOUGH

SIDE

7"

½"

TOP

1¼"

1¼"

10"

CUTS MADE ALONG DASHED LINES

7"

PIZZA DOUGH

PROJECT: LITTLE CAESAR'S CRAZY BREAD

ORIGINATION DATE: 1982

JOB NO. LC897330-CB

LITTLE CAESAR'S CRAZY SAUCE

☆ ♥ ☎ ✏ ✈ ✉ ✂ ☞ ✿

From 1990 to 1993, Little Caesar's sales growth ranked in the top five in the restaurant industry, according to *Nation's Restaurant News* magazine. As of 1993, the company had more than 4,800 outlets raking in $2.3 billion. It's no wonder that founder Michael Ilitch was able to purchase the Detroit Red Wings hockey team in 1982, and then the Detroit Tigers in 1992. Ilitch also owns several arenas and theaters, including the Second City comedy theater in Detroit.

The Crazy Sauce at Little Caesar's is usually served with the Crazy Bread, for dipping. It's a version of pizza sauce, heated in a microwave before you buy it. The sauce can be used with the preceding Crazy Bread recipe, or as a great, fresh sauce for any homemade pizza.

One 15-ounce can tomato puree
¹/₂ teaspoon salt
¹/₄ teaspoon pepper
¹/₄ teaspoon garlic powder

¹/₄ teaspoon dried basil
¹/₄ teaspoon dried marjoram
¹/₄ teaspoon dried oregano
¹/₄ teaspoon ground thyme

1. Combine all the ingredients in an uncovered saucepan over medium heat.
2. When the sauce begins to bubble, reduce the heat and simmer for 30 minutes, stirring often.
3. Remove the sauce from the heat and let it cool. Store in a tightly sealed container in the refrigerator; it will keep for 3 to 4 weeks. Serve hot.

· MAKES 1¹/₂ CUPS

•   •   •   •   •

M&M/MARS ALMOND BAR

☆ ♥ ☎ ✎ ✈ ✉ ✂ ☛ ✿

What started in Tacoma, Washington, in 1911 as a small home-based candy shop has now grown to be one of the largest privately held companies in the world. Mars products are found in more than 100 countries, and the Mars family pulls in revenues in the range of a sweet $11 billion each year.

The Mars Almond Bar was first produced in 1936, when it was known as the Mars Toasted Almond Bar. It was reformulated in 1980 and the name was changed to Mars Bar; in 1990 it was re-named once again, becoming Mars Almond Bar.

You'll need a heavy-duty mixer to handle the nougat in this recipe.

2 cups granulated sugar
$1/2$ cup light corn syrup
$1/2$ cup plus 2 tablespoons water
Pinch salt
2 egg whites

35 unwrapped Kraft caramels
$2/3$ cup whole roasted almonds
Two 12-ounce bags milk chocolate chips

1. In a large saucepan over medium heat, combine the sugar, corn syrup, $1/2$ cup of the water, and the salt. Heat to boiling, then cook using a candy thermometer to monitor the temperature.

2. Beat the egg whites until they are stiff and form peaks. Don't use a plastic bowl for this.

3. When the sugar mixture reaches 270°F, or the *soft-crack stage*, remove from the heat and pour the mixture in thin streams into the egg whites, blending completely with an electric mixer set on low.

4. Continue to mix about 20 minutes, or until the nougat begins to

harden and thickens to the consistency of dough. Mix in the almonds.

5. Press the nougat into a greased 9 × 9-inch pan and chill until firm, about 30 minutes.
6. Melt the caramels with the remaining 2 tablespoons water in a small saucepan over medium heat.

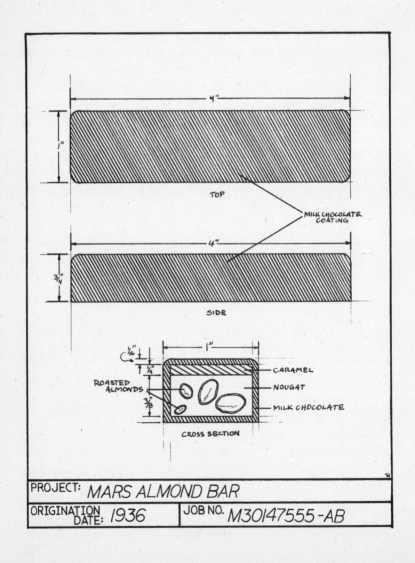

PROJECT: MARS ALMOND BAR

ORIGINATION DATE: 1936   JOB NO. M30147555-AB

7. Pour the caramel over the nougat and return the pan to the refrigerator.

8. When the caramel and nougat are firm (about 30 minutes), slice down the middle of the pan with a sharp knife, and then slice across into 7 segments to make a total of 14 bars.

9. Melt the milk chocolate chips in a microwave for 2 minutes on half power, stirring halfway through the cooking time. Melt completely, but be careful not to overheat.

10. Resting the bar on a fork (and using your fingers if needed), dip each bar into the chocolate to coat completely and tap the fork against the side of the bowl to knock off the excess chocolate. Place on waxed paper and let cool at room temperature until the chocolate is firm, 1 to 2 hours.

MAKES 14 CANDY BARS

• • • •

M&M/MARS
MILKY WAY

☆ ♥ ☎ ✎ ✈ ✉ ✂ ☞ ✿

I find that some people are confused by the brand name M&M/Mars. The company is actually a snack division within the parent company Mars, Incorporated, which produces food products around the world as diverse as Uncle Ben's rice and Kal Kan dog food. When the founder's son, Forrest E. Mars, Sr., returned from England (where he had established the first canned pet food business in that country), he formed a company in Newark, New Jersey, to make small chocolate candies that could be sold throughout the year, not melting in the hot summer months. Those were the first M&M's. The company, called M&M Limited, consolidated with other Mars confectionery businesses in the United States in 1967 to form M&M/Mars as it exists today.

The Mars Milky Way bar was the first chocolate-covered candy bar to find widespread popularity in the United States. It was developed in 1923 by the Mars family, and became so successful so quickly that the company had to build a new manufacturing plant in Chicago just to keep up with demand.

You'll need a heavy-duty mixer for this recipe.

2 cups granulated sugar
1/2 cup light corn syrup
1/2 cup plus 2 tablespoons water
Pinch salt
2 egg whites

35 unwrapped Kraft caramels
1/4 cup semisweet chocolate chips
Two 12-ounce bags milk chocolate chips

1. In a large saucepan over medium heat, combine the sugar, corn syrup, 1/2 cup of the water, and the salt. Stir often until the mixture begins to boil, then continue to cook, using a candy thermometer to monitor the temperature.

2. While the candy boils, beat the egg whites until they are stiff and form peaks. Don't use a plastic bowl for this.
3. When the sugar mixture reaches 270°F, or the *soft-crack stage*, remove from the heat and pour the mixture in thin streams into the egg whites, blending with a mixer set on low speed.
4. Continue to mix for 15 minutes or so. The mixture will thicken as you mix, until it reaches the consistency of cookie dough. At

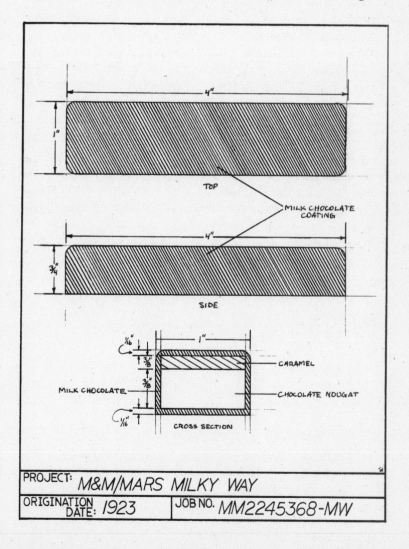

TOP

SIDE

MILK CHOCOLATE COATING

CARAMEL

MILK CHOCOLATE

CHOCOLATE NOUGAT

CROSS SECTION

PROJECT: M&M/MARS MILKY WAY

ORIGINATION DATE: 1923

JOB NO. MM2245368-MW

this point, add the semisweet chocolate chips. Be warned; the mixture will not get any thicker after the chocolate is added, so be sure the candy is very thick and fluffy before adding the chips.

5. When the chocolate chips are completely blended into the candy, press the mixture into a greased 9 × 9-inch pan and refrigerate until cool, about 30 minutes.

6. Heat the caramels with the remaining 2 tablespoons water in a small saucepan until thoroughly melted. Pour the caramel over the refrigerated candy.

7. While the candy cools, melt the milk chocolate chips in the microwave for 2 minutes on medium power. Stir halfway through the heating time. Melt completely, but be careful not to overheat.

8. When the caramel is set, use a sharp knife to cut down the center of the pan. Then cut the candy across into 7 segments, making a total of 14 bars.

9. Resting a bar on a fork (and using your fingers if needed), dip each bar into the chocolate to coat completely, then tap the fork against the side of the bowl to knock off the excess chocolate.

10. Place each bar on waxed paper and cool until firm at room temperature, 1 to 2 hours.

• MAKES 14 CANDY BARS

• • • •

M&M/MARS
3 MUSKETEERS

☆ ♥ ☎ ✎ ✈ ✉ ✂ ☞ ✿

Nougat is an important ingredient in the 3 Musketeers Bar, as well as in many other candy bars created by M&M/Mars. Nougat is made by mixing a hot sugar syrup with whipped egg whites until the solution cools and stiffens, creating a *frappe*. Other ingredients may be added to the nougat during this process to give it different flavors. In this recipe, you'll add chocolate chips to create a dark, chocolaty nougat.

But the 3 Musketeers Bar wasn't always filled with just a chocolate nougat. In fact, when the candy bar was created back in 1932, it was actually three pieces with three flavors: vanilla, strawberry, and chocolate. After World War II, the product was changed to a single chocolate bar because that was the favorite flavor, and customers wanted more of it. Thankfully they didn't decide to change the name to 1 Musketeer!

You'll need a heavy-duty electric mixer for this recipe.

3 cups granulated sugar
³/₄ cup light corn syrup
³/₄ cup water
¹/₈ teaspoon salt

3 egg whites
¹/₃ cup semisweet chocolate chips
Two 12-ounce bags milk chocolate chips

1. In a large saucepan over medium heat, combine the sugar, corn syrup, water, and salt. Heat, stirring, to boiling, then continue to cook, using a candy thermometer to monitor the temperature.
2. Beat the egg whites until they are stiff and form peaks. Don't use a plastic bowl for this.
3. When the sugar solution comes to 270°F, or the *soft-crack stage*, remove from the heat and pour the mixture in thin streams into the egg whites, blending completely with a mixer set on low speed.

4. Continue to mix until the candy begins to harden to the consistency of dough. This may take as long as 20 minutes. At this point, add the semisweet chocolate chips. Remember that the candy *must* already be at the consistency of dough when you add the chocolate; the nougat will thicken no more after the chocolate is added.
5. When the chocolate is thoroughly blended and the nougat has

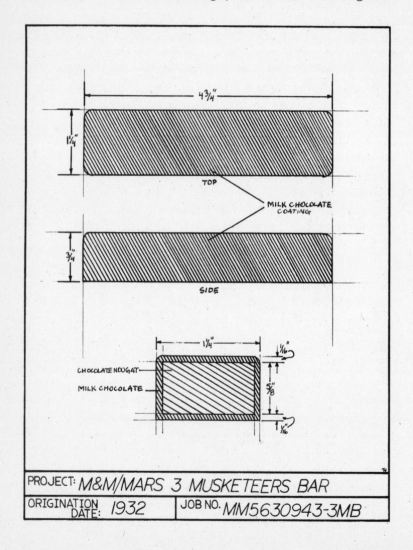

thickened, press it into a greased 9 × 9-inch pan. Refrigerate until firm, about 30 minutes.

6. With a sharp knife, cut the candy in half down the middle of the pan. Then cut across into 7 segments to create a total of 14 bars.

7. Melt the milk chocolate chips in the microwave for 2 minutes on half power, stirring halfway through the heating time. Melt completely, but be careful not to overheat.

8. Resting a bar on a fork (and using your fingers if needed), dip each bar into the chocolate to coat completely and place on wax paper. Cool till firm at room temperature, 1 to 2 hours.

• MAKES 14 CANDY BARS

• • • •

McDONALD'S FILET-O-FISH

☆   ♥   ☎   ✎   ✈   ✉   ✂   ☞   ✿

The year 1963 was a big one in McDonald's history. The 500th McDonald's restaurant opened in Toledo, Ohio, and Hamburger University graduated its 500th student. It was in that same year that McDonald's served its one billionth hamburger in grand fashion on *The Art Linkletter Show*. Ronald McDonald also made his debut that year in Washington, D.C. (one of Willard Scott's earlier jobs—he hasn't changed much). And the Filet-O-Fish sandwich was introduced as the first new menu addition since the restaurant chain opened in 1948.

2 tablespoons mayonnaise
2 teaspoons sweet relish
2 teaspoons minced onion
Pinch salt

2 plain hamburger buns
2 Mrs. Paul's breaded fish portions
    (square)
1 slice American cheese

1. In a small bowl, mix together the mayonnaise, relish, minced onion, and salt and set aside. This is your tartar sauce.
2. Lightly grill the faces of the buns.
3. Cook the fish according to the package instructions. You can bake the fish, but your sandwich will taste much more like the original if you fry it in oil.
4. Divide the tartar sauce and spread it evenly on each of the top buns.
5. Slice the cheese in half and place a piece on each of the bottom buns.
6. Place the cooked fish on top of the cheese slice on each sandwich, and top off the sandwiches with the top buns.
7. Microwave each sandwich on high for 10 seconds.

· MAKES 2 SANDWICHES

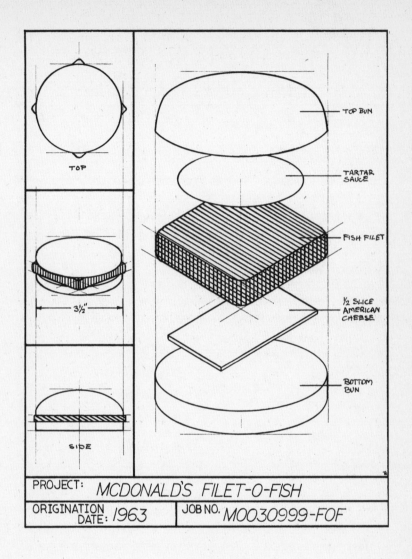

TOP

TOP BUN

TARTAR SAUCE

FISH FILET

½ SLICE AMERICAN CHEESE

BOTTOM BUN

3½"

SIDE

PROJECT: *MCDONALD'S FILET-O-FISH*

ORIGINATION DATE: *1963*

JOB NO. *M0030999-FOF*

TIDBITS

If you can find fish only in wedge shapes, just use two wedges on each sandwich, fitting them together side by side to form a square.

· · · · ·

McDONALD'S HAMBURGER

☆ ♥ ☎ ✎ ✈ ✉ ✂ ☞ ✿

Yes, Ronald McDonald is truly an international hero and celebrity. In Japan, since the "R" sound is not part of the Japanese language, everyone knows the burger-peddling clown as "Donald McDonald." And in Hong Kong, where people place a high value on family relationships, he is called Uncle McDonald, or in their language, "McDonald Suk Suk."

These burgers were the original hallmark of the world's largest fast-food chain. In 1948, when brothers Dick and Mac McDonald opened their first drive-in restaurant in San Bernardino, California, it was this simple sandwich that had hundreds of people driving in from miles around to pick up a sackful for just 15 cents a burger.

¹/₈ pound ground beef
1 plain hamburger bun
Salt to taste
1 tablespoon catsup

¹/₂ teaspoon prepared mustard
¹/₂ teaspoon finely minced onion
1 dill pickle slice

1. Roll the ground beef into a ball and then press flat on wax paper until about ¹/₄ inch thick. You can also prepare the burger ahead of time and freeze it for easier cooking. The burger need not be defrosted before cooking.
2. Brown the faces of the bun in a frying pan over medium heat.
3. Remove the bun and cook the burger in the same pan for 2 minutes per side. Salt both sides during the cooking.
4. On the top bun, spread the catsup, mustard, and onion, in that order, and top with the pickle slice.

5. Put the beef patty on the bottom bun and slap the top and bottom together.
6. Microwave the burger on high for 10 to 15 seconds.

· MAKES 1 HAMBURGER

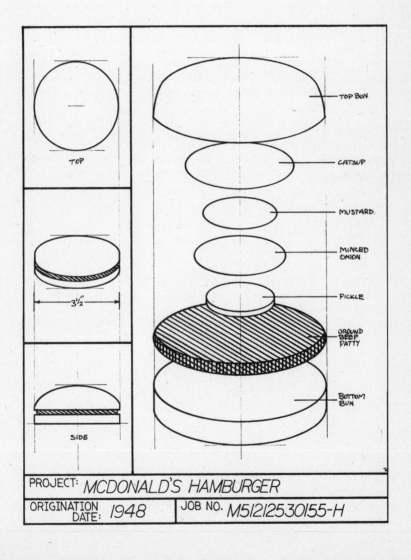

TOP

3½"

SIDE

TOP BUN

CATSUP

MUSTARD

MINCED ONION

PICKLE

GROUND BEEF PATTY

BOTTOM BUN

PROJECT: MCDONALD'S HAMBURGER

ORIGINATION DATE: 1948

JOB NO. M512I2530I55-H

McDonald's Cheeseburger

Follow the recipe above, but add a slice of American cheese (not processed cheese food) on top of the beef patty in the final assembly. Microwave for 15 seconds on high to get that "just out from under the heat lamp" taste.

. . . .

McDONALD'S QUARTER POUNDER (WITH CHEESE)

☆   ♥   ☎   ✎   ✈   ⊠   ✂   ☞   ✿

What is McDonald's sign referring to when it says "Over 100 billion served"? That's not the number of customers served, but actually the number of beef patties sold since McDonald's first opened its doors in the forties. A hamburger counts as one patty. A Big Mac counts as two.

McDonald's sold its 11 billionth hamburger in 1972, the same year that this sandwich, the Quarter Pounder, was added to the growing menu. That was also the year large fries were added and founder Ray Kroc was honored with the Horatio Alger Award (the two events were not related). In 1972, the 2,000th McDonald's opened its doors, and by the end of that year McDonald's had finally become a billion-dollar corporation.

1 sesame-seed bun
1/4 pound ground beef
Salt to taste
1 tablespoon catsup

1/2 teaspoon prepared mustard
1 teaspoon chopped onion
2 dill pickle slices
2 slices American cheese

1. Brown the faces of the bun in a large frying pan over medium heat.
2. Roll the ground beef into a ball and then flatten on wax paper until about 1/4 inch thick.
3. Cook the burger for 3 to 4 minutes per side. Salt each side during the cooking.
4. Spread catsup and then the mustard on the top bun; then add the onion and pickle.

5. Place I slice of cheese on the bottom bun, then the beef patty, then the other slice of cheese.
6. Top off the sandwich with the top bun.
7. Microwave on high for 15 seconds.

- MAKES I BURGER

. . . . .

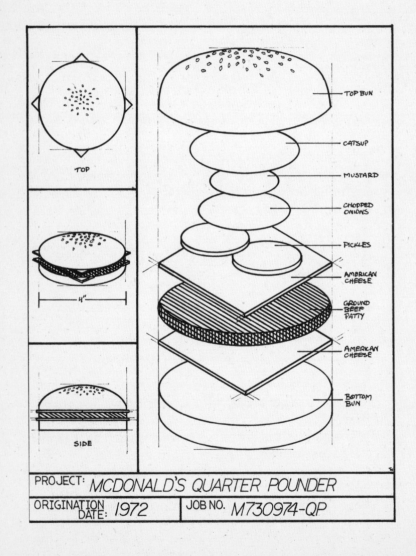

TOP

SIDE

4"

TOP BUN

CATSUP

MUSTARD

CHOPPED ONIONS

PICKLES

AMERICAN CHEESE

GROUND BEEF PATTY

AMERICAN CHEESE

BOTTOM BUN

PROJECT: MCDONALD'S QUARTER POUNDER

ORIGINATION DATE: 1972

JOB NO. M730974-QP

NABISCO CHIPS AHOY!

☆ ♥ ☎ ✎ ✈ ✉ ✂ ☞ ✿

As you bake these cookies, imagine producing a quarter of a million cookies and crackers every minute. That's what Nabisco does—which is why the conglomerate is the largest manufacturer of cookies and crackers in the world. Chips Ahoy! Chocolate Chip Cookies were developed in 1964, along with Chicken In A Biscuit Crackers and Mister Salty Pretzels. But Chips Ahoy! became the big winner for the company. Today it's the world's top-selling chocolate-chip cookie, with more than 6 billion sold every year.

1 1/2 cups vegetable shortening
1 cup packed light brown sugar
1 cup granulated sugar
2 teaspoons salt
1 1/2 teaspoons vanilla extract

1 teaspoon baking soda
4 cups all-purpose flour
1/4 cup water
One 12-ounce bag mini semi-sweet
  chocolate chips

1. Preheat the oven to 325°F.
2. In a large mixing bowl, combine the shortening and sugars and blend with an electric mixer until smooth.
3. Add the salt, vanilla, and baking soda.
4. While beating at low speed, slowly add the flour. Then add the water. Mix thoroughly. Stir in the chocolate chips. Add extra water to dough if needed to make it stick together.
5. Form the cookies by breaking off bits of dough and patting them out with your fingers into 2-inch rounds about 1/8 inch thick.
6. Place the cookies on ungreased cookie sheets and bake for 12 to 18 minutes, or until golden brown on the top and around the edges.

• MAKES ABOUT 3 DOZEN COOKIES

• • • • •

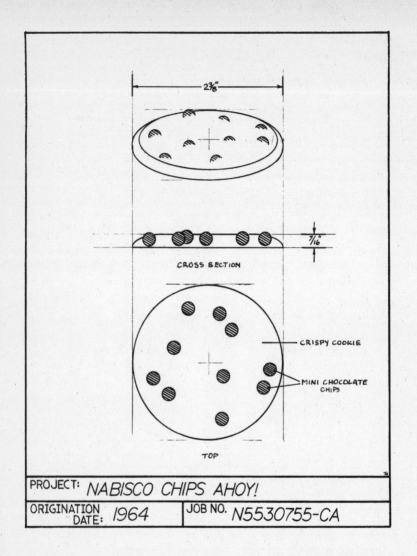

2⅜"

CROSS SECTION

7/16"

CRISPY COOKIE

MINI CHOCOLATE
CHIPS

TOP

PROJECT: *NABISCO CHIPS AHOY!*

ORIGINATION
DATE: *1964*

JOB NO. *N5530755-CA*

NABISCO
NUTTER BUTTER

☆   ♥   ☎   🖉   ✈   ✉   ✂   ☞   ✿

Formerly called the National Biscuit Company, Nabisco was formed in the late 1800s by several bakeries that joined together to meet a growing demand. In the 1870s Nabisco's forefathers had introduced the first individually packaged baked goods. Before this, cookies and crackers had been sold from open barrels or biscuit boxes. The company has become the world's largest manufacturer of cookies and crackers, selling some 42 million packages of Nabisco products each day to retail outlets on every continent.

Nutter Butter Cookies were introduced in 1969 and have quickly taken their place alongside Nabisco's most popular products, including Oreos, Chips Ahoy!, and Fig Newtons.

COOKIES

1/2 cup vegetable shortening	3 tablespoons peanut butter
2/3 cup granulated sugar	1/2 cup old-fashioned Quaker oats
1 egg	1 cup all-purpose flour
1/2 teaspoon salt	

FILLING

1/2 cup peanut butter	1 tablespoon fine graham cracker
3/4 cup powdered sugar	crumbs

1. Preheat the oven to 325°F.
2. In a large bowl, cream together the shortening and sugar with an electric mixer.
3. Add the egg, salt, and peanut butter and beat until well blended.
4. Put the oats in a blender and blend on medium speed until they are almost as finely ground as flour.
5. Add the oats and flour to the mixture and blend well.

6. Pinch out small portions of dough and roll into 1-inch balls in the palm of your hand. Press these flat on ungreased cookie sheets so that they form 2-inch circles. If you're a stickler for a cookie that looks just like the original, you can form the dough into flat peanut shapes similar to those illustrated.
7. Bake for 8 to 10 minutes, or until light brown around the edges.

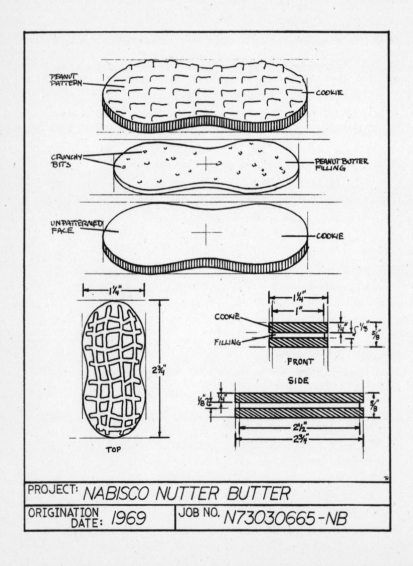

8. While the cookies bake, combine the filling ingredients in a small bowl.
9. When the cookies are cool, use a butter knife to spread a thin layer of filling on the flat side of a cookie and press another on top. Repeat.
- MAKES 2 DOZEN COOKIES

• • • •

NABISCO OREO COOKIE

At one time Nabisco actually conducted a study that determined that 50 percent of Oreo consumers twist the cookie apart before eating it. I guess this is important information, since it concerns the world's top-selling cookie. Historians at Nabisco aren't sure who came up with the idea for this sandwich cookie back in 1912, but they do know that it was introduced along with two other cookie creations that have long since died. The name may have come from the Greek word for mountain, *oreo*, which would once have made sense because the first test version was hill-shaped. When the Oreo was first sold to the public, it was much larger than today's cookie, but it kept shrinking over the years until Nabisco realized it had become much too small and had to enlarge it again to today's current 1³/₄-inch diameter.

In 1975, Nabisco figured we couldn't have too much of a good thing, so the company gave us Double Stuf Oreos, with twice the filling. A smart move. Today Double Stuf holds its own rank as the fifth most popular cookie in America.

COOKIE

One 18.25-ounce Duncan Hines
   Dark Dutch Fudge cake mix

¹/₃ cup water
2 tablespoons shortening

FILLING

3³/₄ cups powdered sugar
¹/₂ tablespoon granulated sugar
¹/₂ teaspoon vanilla extract

¹/₂ cup shortening
2 tablespoons hot water

1. Preheat the oven to 325°F.
2. Blend all the cookie ingredients with an electric mixer; then

knead with your hands until it reaches the consistency of dough.

3. Form the dough into balls about ¾ inch in diameter and press flat ½ inch apart on greased cookie sheets. Bake for 6 to 8 minutes, or until the cookies are crunchy.

4. Let the cookies cool on the sheets.

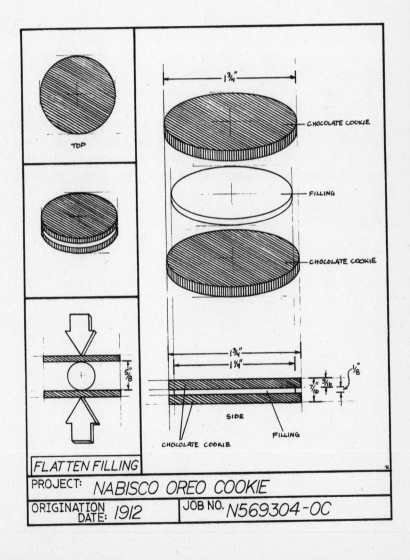

TOP

CHOCOLATE COOKIE

FILLING

CHOCOLATE COOKIE

SIDE

CHOCOLATE COOKIE

FILLING

FLATTEN FILLING

PROJECT: NABISCO OREO COOKIE

ORIGINATION DATE: 1912

JOB NO. N569304-OC

5. As the cookies cool, combine the filling ingredients well with an electric mixer.
6. With your hands form the filling into balls about ½ to ¾ inch in diameter.
7. Place a filling ball in the center of the flat side of a cooled cookie and press with another cookie, flat side down, until the filling spreads to the edge.

- MAKES 60 COOKIES

TIDBITS

This may be obvious to you, but you can expand your own home-made line of Oreos by creating your own versions of Double Stuf® or the giant Oreos called Oreo Big Stuf®. Just add twice the filling for Double Stuf, or make the cookie twice the size for Big Stuf. Go crazy. Try Triple Stuf or Quadruple Stuf or Quintuple Stuf . . . somebody stop me.

· · · ·

NESTLÉ CRUNCH

☆　♥　☎　✎　✈　✉　✂　☛　✿

In 1867, infant mortality rates in Vevey, Switzerland, had been climbing and Henri Nestlé was working hard on a concoction of concentrated milk, sugar, and cereal for babies who were refusing their mother's milk. Eventually he discovered a formula that helped infants to stay strong and healthy. He called his new product Farine Lactée and merged with two American brothers, Charles and George Page, who had come to Switzerland to capitalize on Swiss canned milk technology. Their new company was called Nestlé & Anglo-Swiss Condensed Milk Company, and quickly expanded into fifteen other countries. Seven years later, Nestlé sold the company to three local businessmen for one million francs.

The new company kept the Nestlé name and started selling chocolate in 1904. In 1929, the company acquired Cailler, the first company to mass-produce chocolate bars, and Swiss General, the company credited with inventing milk chocolate. This company was the core of the chocolate business as we know it today. The Nestlé Crunch bar was introduced in 1928 and is now the company's top-selling candy bar.

Two 12-ounce bags milk chocolate chips (Nestlé is best)

1½ cups Rice Krispies

1. Melt the chocolate chips in a microwave-safe bowl in a microwave set on medium for 2 minutes. Stir halfway through the heating time. Melt thoroughly, but be careful not to overheat.
2. Gently mix the Rice Krispies into the chocolate and pour into a greased 9 × 12-inch pan.
3. Slam the pan on the counter or floor to level the chocolate.
4. Refrigerate until firm, about 30 minutes.

5. Cut the candy in half widthwise and then cut it twice lengthwise, making 6 bars.

· MAKES 6 KING-SIZE BARS

. . . .

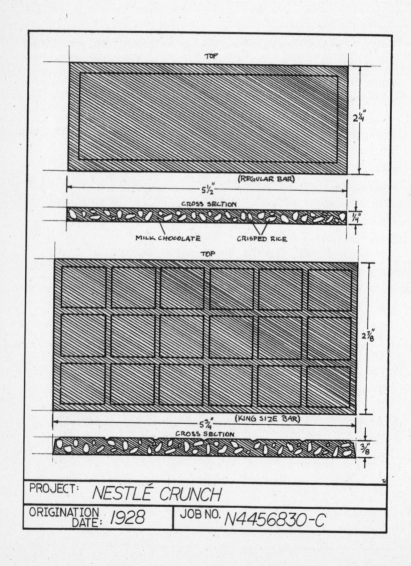

TOP

(REGULAR BAR)

2¼"

5½"

CROSS SECTION

¼"

MILK CHOCOLATE   CRISPED RICE

TOP

2⅞"

(KING SIZE BAR)

5¾"

CROSS SECTION

⅜"

PROJECT: *NESTLÉ CRUNCH*

ORIGINATION DATE: *1928*

JOB NO. *N4456830-C*

NESTLÉ
100 GRAND BAR

Nestlé is the world's largest packaged food manufacturer, coffee roaster, and chocolate maker. It is the largest single company in Switzerland today, but Nestlé derives only 2 percent of its revenue from its home country.

The company is quite diverse. Nestlé's product lines include beverages and drinks, chocolate and candy, dairy products, and frozen foods. The company also operates more than thirty Stouffer Hotels and owns 25 percent of the French cosmetics giant L'Oréal. In the United States, where the company is called Nestlé USA, it ranks third behind Mars, Inc., and Hershey USA in chocolate sales.

This candy bar was introduced in 1966 as the $100,000 Bar, then its name was changed to 100 Grand Bar in 1985.

30 unwrapped Kraft caramels, at   *³/₄ cup Rice Krispies*
*   room temperature*
One 12-ounce bag milk chocolate chips

1. With your fingers, flatten each caramel into a rectangle about ¼ inch thick.
2. Melt the chocolate chips in a microwave-safe bowl in a microwave set on half power for 2 minutes. Stir halfway through the heating time. Melt thoroughly, but do not overheat.
3. Add the Rice Krispies and stir just until blended.
4. Dip each caramel into the chocolate to coat completely and then place on waxed paper. Cool until firm at room temperature, 1 to 2 hours.

• MAKES 30 CANDY BARS

· · · ·

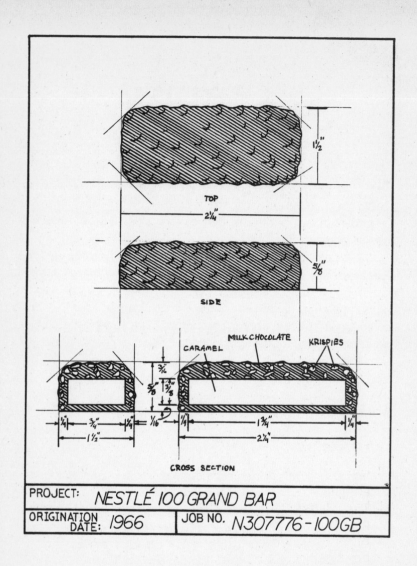

TOP

$1\frac{1}{2}''$

$2\frac{1}{4}''$

SIDE

$\frac{5}{8}''$

CROSS SECTION

CARAMEL

MILK CHOCOLATE

KRISPIES

$\frac{3}{16}''$

$\frac{5}{8}''$ $\frac{3}{8}''$

$\frac{1}{4}''$ $\frac{3}{4}''$ $\frac{1}{4}''$ $\frac{1}{16}''$ $\frac{1}{4}''$ $1\frac{3}{4}''$ $\frac{1}{4}''$

$1\frac{1}{2}''$ $2\frac{1}{4}''$

PROJECT:	NESTLÉ 100 GRAND BAR	
ORIGINATION DATE:	1966	JOB NO. N307776-100GB

POPEYE'S
FAMOUS
FRIED CHICKEN

☆　♥　☎　✎　✈　✉　✂　☛　✿

Popeye's Famous Fried Chicken & Biscuits has become the third largest quick-service chicken chain in the world in the twenty-two years since its first store opened in New Orleans in 1972. (KFC has the number-one slot, followed by Church's Chicken.) Since then, the chain has grown to 813 units, with many of them overseas in Germany, Japan, Jamaica, Honduras, Guam, and Korea.

I picked this recipe because the chicken has a unique Cajun-style spiciness. See what you think.

6 cups vegetable oil
2/3 cup all-purpose flour
1 tablespoon salt
2 tablespoons white pepper

1 teaspoon cayenne pepper
2 teaspoons paprika
3 eggs
1 frying chicken with skin, cut up

1. Heat the oil over medium heat in a deep fryer or in a wide, deep pan on the stove.
2. In a large, shallow bowl, combine the flour, salt, peppers, and paprika.
3. Break the eggs into a separate shallow bowl and beat until blended.
4. Check the oil by dropping in a pinch of the flour mixture. If the oil bubbles rapidly around the flour, it is ready.
5. Dip each piece of chicken into the eggs, then coat generously with the flour mixture. Drop each piece into the hot oil and fry for 15 to 25 minutes, or until it is a dark golden brown.
6. Remove the chicken to paper towels or a rack to drain.

· MAKES 8 PIECES

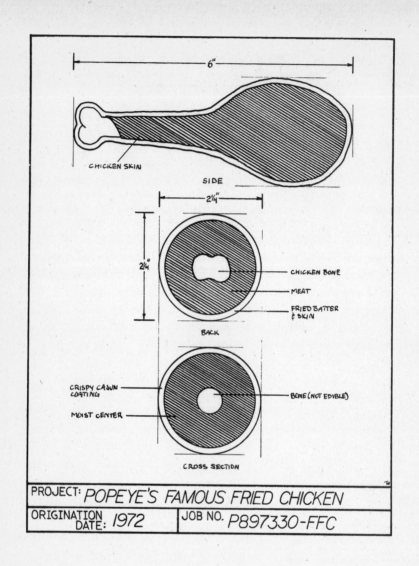

6"

CHICKEN SKIN

SIDE

2¼"

2¼"

CHICKEN BONE

MEAT

FRIED BATTER
& SKIN

BACK

CRISPY CAJUN
COATING

BONE (NOT EDIBLE)

MOIST CENTER

CROSS SECTION

PROJECT: POPEYE'S FAMOUS FRIED CHICKEN

ORIGINATION
DATE: 1972

JOB NO. P897330-FFC

POPEYE'S RED BEANS AND RICE

☆   ♥   ☎   ✎   ✈   ✉   ✄   ☛   ✿

If there isn't a Popeye's Famous Chicken & Biscuits outlet near you, there probably will be sometime soon. Popeye's now has restaurants in thirty-eight states and is growing impressively. With a name like Popeye's, you would expect something with spinach in it, but instead you'll find a selection of Cajun-spiced fare including this tasty combination of white rice and red beans. I know many people who go to Popeye's just for a sixteen-ounce cup of Red Beans and Rice, and I've now become one of them.

BEANS
One 30-ounce can or two 15-ounce
    cans small red beans
1 1/2 teaspoons white pepper

1/4 teaspoon paprika
4 tablespoons (1/2 stick) butter
1/4 teaspoon garlic powder

RICE
1 1/2 cups quick-cooking rice (Minute
    Rice or Uncle Ben's)
1 1/2 cups water

2 tablespoons (1/4 stick) butter
1/2 teaspoon garlic salt

1. Pour the beans with their liquid into a large saucepan. Turn the heat to medium.
2. Add the pepper, paprika, butter, and garlic powder.
3. When the beans begin to boil, use a fork to mash some of them against the side of the pan. Stir the mixture constantly. In about 20 minutes, the beans will reach the consistency of refried beans

(in other words, they will have a smooth, creamy texture with some whole beans still swimming around).

4. Prepare the rice, using the 2 tablespoons butter and ½ teaspoon garlic salt instead of the butter and salt amounts specified on the box for 4 servings.

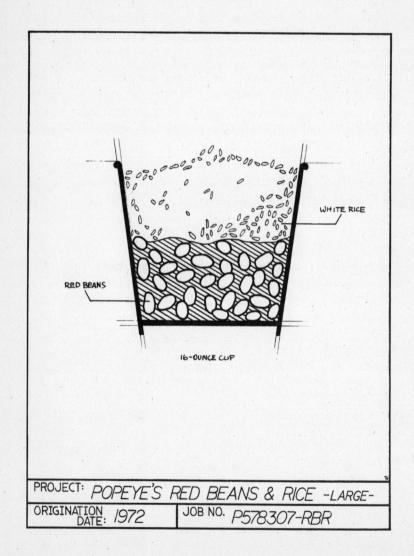

WHITE RICE

RED BEANS

16-OUNCE CUP

PROJECT: *POPEYE'S RED BEANS & RICE* -LARGE-

ORIGINATION DATE: *1972* JOB NO. *P578307-RBR*

5. To serve, pour $^1/_2$ cup of beans into a bowl and scoop the same amount of rice on top of the beans.

•   SERVES 4

•   •   •   •

SNAPPLE
ICED TEA

☆ ♥ ☎ ✎ ✈ ✉ ✂ ☛ ✿

In 1972, brothers-in-law Leonard Marsh and Hyman Golden had become tired of running a window-washing business. They contacted their friend Arnold Greenberg and told him they wanted to start selling bottled fruit juices. Greenberg had a health-food store and thought their idea for all-natural beverages was a good one, so together they started selling pure fruit juices under the name Unadulterated Food Products. It took the trio about a decade to acquire the name they really wanted, Snapple, for $500 from a guy in Texas who had used it on an apple soda that bombed. Snapple's big break came in 1988, when the company started bottling ready-to-drink iced teas. It took only five years for Snapple to become the leader in the iced tea market, blowing away giants Lipton and Nestea. The Snapple iced tea phenomenon helped the company increase sales between 1988 and 1992 by nearly 1,300 percent. Whew.

LEMON

2 quarts (8 cups) water
3 Lipton tea bags (orange pekoe
    and pekoe cut black tea blend)

³/₄ cup granulated sugar or one
    16-ounce bottle light corn syrup
¹/₃ cup plus 1 tablespoon lemon
    juice

DIET LEMON

2 quarts (8 cups) water
3 Lipton tea bags (orange pekoe
    and pekoe cut black tea blend)

Twelve 1-gram envelopes Sweet'n
    Low or Equal sweetener
¹/₃ cup plus 1 tablespoon lemon juice

ORANGE

2 quarts (8 cups) water
3 Lipton tea bags (orange pekoe
    and pekoe cut black tea blend)
$^3/_4$ cup granulated sugar or one 16-
    ounce bottle light corn syrup

$^1/_3$ cup lemon juice
$^1/_8$ teaspoon orange extract

STRAWBERRY

2 quarts (8 cups) water
3 Lipton tea bags (orange pekoe
    and pekoe cut black tea blend)
$^3/_4$ cup granulated sugar or one 16-
    ounce bottle light corn syrup

$^1/_3$ cup plus 1 tablespoon lemon juice
1 tablespoon strawberry extract

CRANBERRY

2 quarts (8 cups) water
3 Lipton tea bags (orange pekoe
    and pekoe cut black tea blend)
$^3/_4$ cup granulated sugar or one 16-
    ounce bottle light corn syrup

$^1/_3$ cup plus 2 tablespoons lemon
    juice
2 tablespoons Ocean Spray cran-
    berry juice cocktail concentrate

1. For any of the flavors, boil the water in a large saucepan.
2. When the water comes to a rapid boil, turn off the heat, put the tea bags into the water, and cover.
3. After the tea has steeped about 1 hour, pour the sugar or sweetener into a 2-quart pitcher; then add the tea. The tea should still be warm, so the sugar or sweetener will dissolve easily.
4. Add the flavoring ingredients (plus additional water if needed to bring the tea to the 2-quart line). Chill.

·   MAKES 2 QUARTS

·   ·   ·   ·

STARK MARY JANE

☆ ♥ ☎ ✎ ✈ ✉ ✄ ☛ ✿

In 1914, Charles H. Miller came up with this molasses and peanut butter candy and named it after his favorite aunt. His candy company flourished, selling many confections, but none as popular as the Mary Jane. Eventually all the other candies were eliminated and Mary Janes came to be the only candy produced by the Miller company. Miller tried playing with the formula to improve the candy, but none could compare to the original. In 1985, Stark Candy Company bought the Miller company and added the Stark name to the wrapper. The candy is much the same today as it was eighty years ago.

1 cup granulated sugar	1 egg white
1 cup light corn syrup	1/2 cup peanut butter
1/2 cup water	1/4 cup powdered sugar
3 tablespoons molasses	Cornstarch for dusting

1. Combine the sugar, corn syrup, and water in a saucepan over medium heat.
2. Heat, stirring, until the sugar begins to boil, then continue to cook, using a candy thermometer to monitor the temperature.
3. When the sugar reaches 240°F, or the *soft-ball stage*, beat the egg white in a microwave-safe bowl until it is stiff and forms peaks. Divide the beaten egg white, and throw out half. (We only need 1/2 egg white for this recipe, and it is easier to divide when beaten.)
4. When the sugar reaches 265°F, or the *hard-ball stage*, stir in the molasses, then pour the mixture in thin streams into the egg white while beating with an electric mixer on low speed.
5. Beat for 3 to 4 minutes and then pour half the mixture into a

9 × 9-inch greased pan and let it firm up in the refrigerator for 5 to 10 minutes.

6. Combine the peanut butter and powdered sugar.
7. When the candy is firm, spread a thin layer of the peanut butter mixture on top.

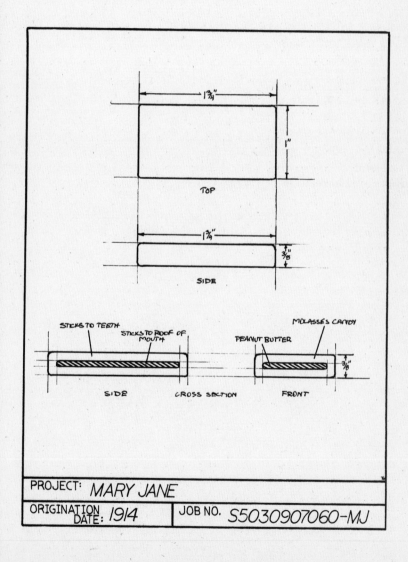

TOP

SIDE

STICKS TO TEETH
STICKS TO ROOF OF MOUTH
MOLASSES CANDY
PEANUT BUTTER

SIDE
CROSS SECTION
FRONT

PROJECT: *MARY JANE*

ORIGINATION DATE: *1914*   JOB NO. *S5030907060-MJ*

8. Microwave the remaining candy mixture for 1 minute on high, or until it becomes soft again.

9. Pour the softened candy over the peanut butter layer.

10. When the candy is cool but still pliable, (about 20 minutes later) turn it out onto a surface dusted lightly with cornstarch. Use a cornstarch-dusted rolling pin to roll the candy about $1/4$ inch thick.

11. Use kitchen scissors or a sharp knife to cut the candy into $1\frac{1}{2}$ × $1/2$-inch rectangles.

- MAKES 30 CANDIES

• • • •

STRAWBERRY JULIUS AND PINEAPPLE JULIUS

☆ ♥ ☎ ✎ ✈ ✉ ✂ ☞ _ ✿

In the first *Top Secret Recipes*, I included a recipe for homemade Orange Julius that was often requested for demonstrations on TV talk shows. Just about every time I did the demonstration I was asked how to make two other Julius flavors, and I wished I had included them as well. So here they are: strawberry and pineapple. Both are made like the orange version but have chunks of real fruit thrown in, just like the real things.

1 cup frozen sliced strawberries, thawed, or one 8-ounce can crushed pineapple in juice
1 cup water

2 egg whites
$^3/_4$ teaspoon vanilla extract
$^1/_4$ cup granulated sugar
1 heaping cup crushed ice

Combine all the ingredients in a blender set on high speed for exactly 1 minute.

- MAKES 2 DRINKS

TIDBITS

For the Strawberry Julius, sweetened sliced strawberries work best. They can often be found in 16-ounce boxes in the frozen-food section of the supermarket. Make sure to thaw them first.

• • • • •

SUPER PRETZELS

☆ ♥ ☎ ✎ ✈ ✉ ✂ ☞ ❀

Gerry Shreiber, a college dropout, wasn't happy with the metal-working business he had been operating for about seven years with a friend, so the two decided to sell out. Shreiber's take was about $60,000, but he needed a new job. By chance one day, he wandered into a Philadelphia waterbed store and struck up a conversation with an investor in a troubled soft pretzel company. After touring the rundown plant, Shreiber thought he could turn the company around, so he put his money to work and bought J&J Soft Pretzels for $72,100. That was in 1971. At the time, J&J had at least ten competitors in the soft pretzel business, but over the years Shreiber devised a strategy that would eliminate this competition and help his company grow—he simply bought most of them out.

Today J&J Super Pretzels are uncontested in the frozen soft pretzel market, and they currently constitute about 70 percent of the soft pretzels that are sold in the country's malls, convenience stores, amusement parks, stadiums, and movie theaters.

One $1/4$-ounce package active dry
   yeast
1 cup warm water (105 to 110°F)
$3^3/4$ cups all-purpose flour
3 tablespoons light corn syrup
2 tablespoons ($1/4$ stick) butter, softened

1 teaspoon salt
4 cups cold water
$1/3$ cup baking soda
Coarse pretzel salt (such as kosher
   salt)

1. Dissolve the yeast in the warm water in a large bowl.
2. Add 2 cups of the flour and beat until smooth.
3. Add the corn syrup, butter, and salt, and mix well about 2 minutes.

4. Add the remaining flour and knead with your hands until all the flour is worked into the dough.
5. Cover the bowl and set the dough in a warm, cozy place where it can ponder the meaning of "Rise, you gooey glob!" Allow the dough to double in size, from 1 to 1½ hours.
6. Remove the dough from the bowl and divide into 10 equal pieces.

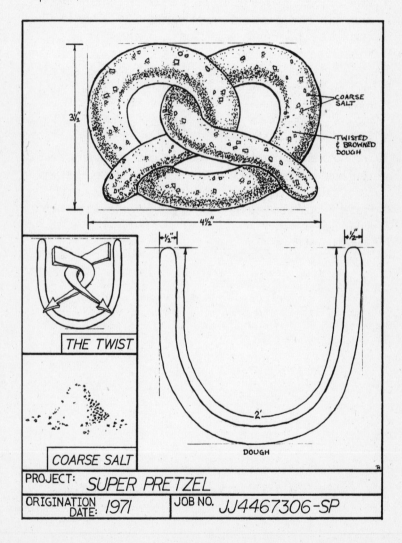

3½"

4½"

COARSE SALT

TWISTED & BROWNED DOUGH

THE TWIST

COARSE SALT

½"   ½"

2'

DOUGH

PROJECT: SUPER PRETZEL

ORIGINATION DATE: 1971   JOB NO. JJ4467306-SP

7. With your hands, roll each piece of dough out on a flat surface until it's about 2 feet long.

8. Holding the dough at both ends, give each strip of dough a twist. Lay the twists well spaced on greased cookie sheets (refer to the illustration for design specifics). Let these rise for another 30 to 45 minutes.

9. When the dough has nearly doubled again, combine the cold water and baking soda in a large saucepan and bring to a boil. This will be your browning solution (a.k.a. *caustic bath*).

10. Preheat the oven to 350°F.

11. Drop each pretzel, one at a time, into the boiling solution. Soak each pretzel for 1 minute, carefully turning after 30 seconds. Return to the cookie sheets.

12. Bake the pretzels for 12 to 15 minutes, or until they are golden brown.

13. Eat the pretzels hot or allow them to cool and freeze them. If you want salt, lightly moisten the surface of the pretzel with a pastry brush and apply a generous sprinkling of coarse salt.

14. Frozen pretzels can be reheated in a microwave set on high for about 30 seconds.

MAKES 10 PRETZELS

• • • •

TACO BELL
HOT
TACO SAUCE

☆ ♥ ☎ ✎ ✈ ✉ ✂ ☞ ✿

You can't buy it in grocery stores, so if you want a substantial portion of Taco Bell's great Taco Sauce to smother your own creations in, you'll have to collect pocketfuls of those little blister packs. But that would be mooching. So here's a way to make plenty of hot sauce just like the stuff people are pouring over the 4 million tacos served at 4,200 Taco Bell restaurants in forty states and around the world every day.

One 6-ounce can tomato paste
3 cups water
2 teaspoons cayenne pepper
1½ tablespoons chili powder
2½ teaspoons salt

2 teaspoons cornstarch
2 teaspoons distilled white vinegar
1 tablespoon minced dried onion
2 tablespoons canned jalapeño
    slices ("nacho slices")

1. Combine the tomato paste with the water in a saucepan over medium heat. Stir until smooth.
2. Add the cayenne pepper, chili powder, salt, cornstarch, vinegar, and dried onion and stir.
3. Chop the jalapeño slices very fine. You can use a food processor, but don't puree. The best kind of jalapeños to use are those bottled for nachos or pizza. Add them to the mixture.
4. Heat the mixture to boiling. Continue to stir about 3 minutes and remove from the heat.
5. Let the sauce stand until cool, and then put in a tightly sealed container and refrigerate. This will last for 1 to 2 months.
- MAKES 3½ CUPS

· · · ·

TASTYKAKE CHOCOLATE CUPCAKES

☆　♥　☎　✎　✈　✉　✂　☞　✿

In 1914, the founders of the Tasty Baking Company set out to create "the cake that made Mother stop baking." The idea of small, prewrapped cakes made fresh at the bakery and delivered to local grocery stores was especially appealing back then. Tastykake products remain popular; every day the company ships and sells millions of Tastykake products. Perhaps the success of the product over the years lies in the secret recipes that have gone remarkably unchanged since they were first created. These chocolate cupcakes in several varieties are the company's top-selling item, with more than 7 million baked weekly.

You'll need a pastry bag to make the filled variety.

CUPCAKES
One 18.25-ounce box Duncan Hines Moist Deluxe Devil's Food cake mix

3 eggs
$1/2$ cup vegetable oil
$1^1/3$ cups water

CHOCOLATE ICING
$5^1/3$ tablespoons ($2/3$ stick) butter, softened
$1/2$ cup semisweet chocolate chips

$1^1/2$ teaspoons vanilla extract
1 tablespoon milk
$2^1/4$ cups powdered sugar

BUTTERCREAM ICING
$5^1/3$ tablespoons ($2/3$ stick) butter, softened
$1^1/2$ teaspoons vanilla extract

$2^1/2$ tablespoons milk
$1/8$ teaspoon salt
3 cups powdered sugar

FILLING

¹/₂ cup shortening	Pinch salt
¹/₂ teaspoon vanilla extract	I cup powdered sugar

1. Preheat the oven to 350°F.
2. Make the cupcakes according to the directions on the box of

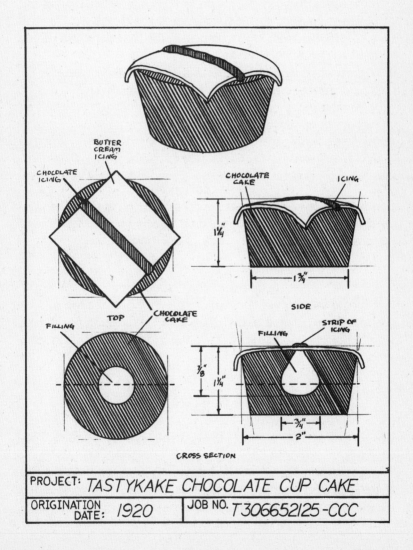

BUTTER CREAM ICING

CHOCOLATE ICING

CHOCOLATE CAKE

ICING

1¼"

1¾"

SIDE

TOP

CHOCOLATE CAKE

FILLING

STRIP OF ICING

FILLING

⅞"

1¼"

¾"

2"

CROSS SECTION

PROJECT: TASTYKAKE CHOCOLATE CUP CAKE

ORIGINATION DATE: 1920

JOB NO. T306652125-CCC

cake mix. (Combine the ingredients, mix for 2 minutes, pour into lightly greased muffin cups, and bake for 19 to 22 minutes.)

3. While the cupcakes bake, make the chocolate and/or buttercream icings.

Chocolate icing: In a mixing bowl, combine the butter with the chocolate chips melted in a microwave set on high for 30 to 45 seconds. Blend in the vanilla, milk, and powdered sugar and beat with an electric mixer until smooth and creamy.

Buttercream icing: Combine all the ingredients in a mixing bowl and beat until smooth.

4. If you're making the filled cupcakes, combine the ingredients for the filling in another mixing bowl and beat until fluffy.

5. When the cupcakes are cool, complete each by following the directions below for your preference.

• MAKES 24 CUPCAKES

Chocolate-Iced Cupcakes

First spread a layer of chocolate frosting on each cupcake. Then, using a pastry bag with a small, round tip, draw a single straight line of buttercream icing down the middle of the chocolate icing.

Buttercream-Iced Cupcakes

First spread a layer of buttercream icing evenly over the top of each cupcake. Then, using a pastry bag with a small, round tip, draw a straight line of chocolate icing down the middle of the buttercream icing.

Creme-Filled Cupcakes

If it's filled cupcakes you want, you need to fill them before you spread on the frosting. How do you do this? It's really very easy.

Use a toothpick or wooden skewer to make a hole in the top of the unfrosted cupcake. Stick the toothpick into the middle of the cupcake and then swirl it around to carve out a cavity in the middle of the cake. This is where the filling will go.

Use a pastry bag to inject a small amount (about 1 teaspoon) of filling into each cupcake, to fill the hole. When you ice your cupcakes, the icing will neatly hide the hole you made.

· · · ·

WENDY'S GRILLED CHICKEN FILLET SANDWICH

☆ ♥ ☎ ✎ ✈ ✉ ✂ ☞ ✿

In 1990, Wendy's not only added this new sandwich to its growing menu, but also added more international restaurants to the chain, including stores in Indonesia, Greece, Turkey, and Guatemala. Wendy's now claims more than 4,000 outlets around the world, with more than $3 billion in sales.

This is an excellent sandwich if you like grilled chicken, and it contains only nine grams of fat, if you're counting.

1 plain hamburger bun
1/2 skinned, boneless chicken breast
Salt to taste

1 tablespoon Wishbone Honey Dijon
    salad dressing
1 lettuce leaf
1 large tomato slice

1. Heat the grill or broiler to medium heat.
2. Brown the faces of the bun in a frying pan over medium heat.
3. Cook the chicken breast for 6 to 10 minutes per side, or until done. Salt each side during the cooking.
4. Spread the salad dressing on the top bun.
5. Place the cooked chicken on the bottom bun. Top with the lettuce leaf, tomato slice, and top bun, in that order.
6. Microwave on high for 15 seconds.
· MAKES 1 SANDWICH

· · · ·

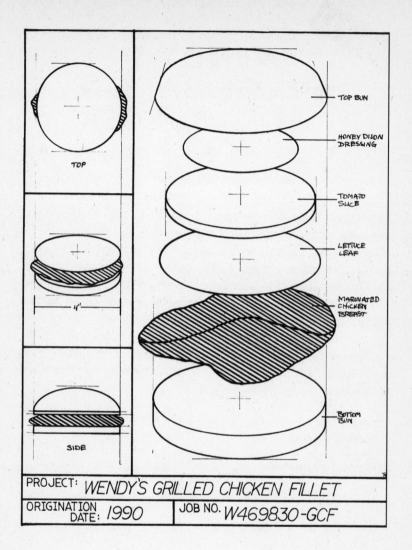

TOP

4"

SIDE

TOP BUN

HONEY DIJON DRESSING

TOMATO SLICE

LETTUCE LEAF

MARINATED CHICKEN BREAST

BOTTOM BUN

PROJECT: WENDY'S GRILLED CHICKEN FILLET

ORIGINATION DATE: 1990

JOB NO. W469830-GCF

WENDY'S JUNIOR BACON CHEESEBURGER

☆　♥　☎　✎　✈　✉　✂　☛　✿

Surely when Dave Thomas opened his first Wendy's Old Fashioned Hamburgers restaurant in 1969 and named it after his daughter, he never imagined the tremendous success and growth his hamburger chain would realize. He also could not have known that in 1989 he would begin starring in a series of television ads that would give Wendy's the biggest customer awareness level since its famous "Where's the beef?" campaign.

In that same year, Wendy's introduced the Super Value Menu, a selection of items all priced under a buck. The Junior Bacon Cheeseburger was added to the selection of inexpensive items and quickly became a hit.

1 plain hamburger bun	1 slice American cheese
1/3 pound ground beef	2 strips cooked bacon
Salt to taste	1 lettuce leaf
1 tablespoon mayonnaise	1 tomato slice

1. Brown the faces of the bun in a frying pan over medium heat. Keep the pan hot.
2. Form the ground beef into a square patty approximately 4 × 4 inches.
3. Cook the patty in the pan for 3 to 4 minutes per side, or until done. Salt each side during the cooking.
4. Spread the mayonnaise on the top bun.
5. Place the patty on the bottom bun. On top, stack the cheese, bacon (side by side), lettuce leaf and tomato slice, in that order. Top off with the top bun.

• MAKES 1 BURGER

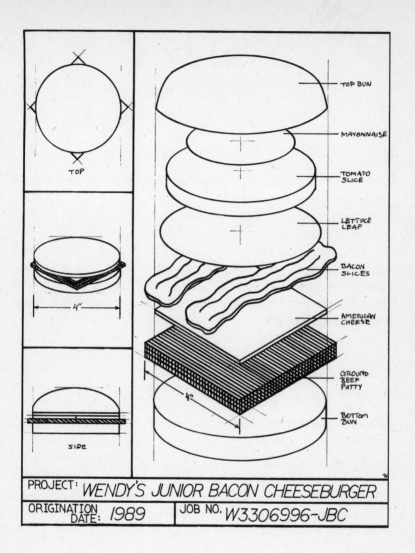

TOP

4"

SIDE

TOP BUN

MAYONNAISE

TOMATO SLICE

LETTUCE LEAF

BACON SLICES

AMERICAN CHEESE

GROUND BEEF PATTY

BOTTOM BUN

4"

PROJECT: *WENDY'S JUNIOR BACON CHEESEBURGER*

ORIGINATION DATE: *1989*

JOB NO. *W3306996-JBC*

WENDY'S
SINGLE

☆　　♥　　☎　　✎　　✈　　✉　　✄　　☛　　✿

In 1984, the diminutive Clara Peller blurted out in a series of four television ads the memorable phrase that would pop up on T-shirts and in presidential campaigns: "Where's the beef?" The ad was devised by Wendy's advertising agency to attack the misconception that its Single hamburger was smaller than its competitors' "big name" hamburgers. The campaign was so original that it stole the show at the 1984 Clio Awards, winning the advertising industry's highest honors and registering the highest consumer awareness level in the industry's history.

1 plain hamburger bun	1/2 teaspoon prepared mustard
1/4 pound ground beef	1 lettuce leaf
Salt to taste	3 raw onion rings
1 teaspoon catsup	1 large tomato slice
1 tablespoon mayonnaise	3 to 4 dill pickle slices

1. Brown the faces of the bun in a large frying pan over medium heat. Keep the pan hot.
2. On wax paper, shape the ground beef into an approximately 4 × 4-inch square. It's best to freeze this patty ahead of time for easier cooking. Don't defrost before cooking.
3. Cook the burger in the pan for 3 minutes per side, or until done. Salt both sides during the cooking.
4. Spread the catsup and then the mayonnaise on the top bun.
5. Put the cooked patty on the bottom bun. On top of the meat, spread the mustard, then place the lettuce, onion, tomato, and pickles, in that order.
6. Top off with the top bun and microwave for 15 seconds.
- MAKES 1 BURGER

Single with Cheese

For a Single with cheese, place 1 slice of American cheese (not processed cheese food) on the beef patty when assembling the burger.

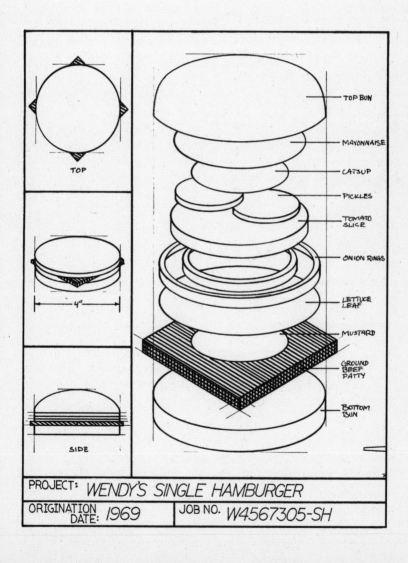

TOP

4"

SIDE

TOP BUN

MAYONNAISE

CATSUP

PICKLES

TOMATO SLICE

ONION RINGS

LETTUCE LEAF

MUSTARD

GROUND BEEF PATTY

BOTTOM BUN

PROJECT: WENDY'S SINGLE HAMBURGER

ORIGINATION DATE: 1969

JOB NO. W4567305-SH

Double and Double with Cheese

Make this burger the same way as the Single, but stack another patty on the first one so that you have a total of $1/2$ pound ground beef.

If you want a Double with cheese, put one slice of cheese between the two beef patties.

. . . .

WHITE CASTLE BURGERS

☆ ♥ ☎ ✎ ✈ ✉ ✂ ☜ ✿

Nicknamed "Sliders" and "Gut Bombers," these famous tiny burgers were one of the earliest fast-food creations. It all started in 1921 when E. W. Ingram borrowed $700 to open a hamburger stand in Wichita, Kansas. He was able to pay the loan back within ninety days. Ingram chose the name White Castle because "white" signified purity and cleanliness, while "castle" represented strength, permanence, and stability. White Castle lived up to its name, maintaining permanence and stability by growing steadily over the years to a total of 275 restaurants.

Ingram's inspiration was the development of steam-grilling, a unique process that helps the burgers retain moisture. The secret is simply to grill the meat over a small pile of onions. Five holes in each burger help to ensure thorough cooking without having to flip the patties.

Today customers can still buy these burgers "by the sack" at the outlets, or pick them up in the freezer section of most grocery stores.

1 pound ground beef	Salt to taste
8 hot-dog buns or 16 hamburger buns	Pepper to taste
	American cheese (optional)
1/2 medium onion	Pickle slices (optional)

1. Prepare the beef ahead of time by separating into sixteen 1-ounce portions and flattening each on wax paper into very thin square patties, about 2 1/2 inches on a side. Using a small circular object like the tip of a pen cap, make five small, evenly spaced holes in each patty. Freeze the patties (still on the wax paper) completely and you're ready to cook.

2. If you're using hot-dog buns, cut off the ends and then cut each bun in half to make 2 buns from each. If you're using hamburger buns, cut each down to about a 2½-inch square.
3. Slice the onion into match-size pieces.
4. Grill the faces of the buns in a large pan over medium heat.
5. In the hot pan, spread out tablespoon-size piles of onions 3 inches apart. Salt and pepper each pile of onions.

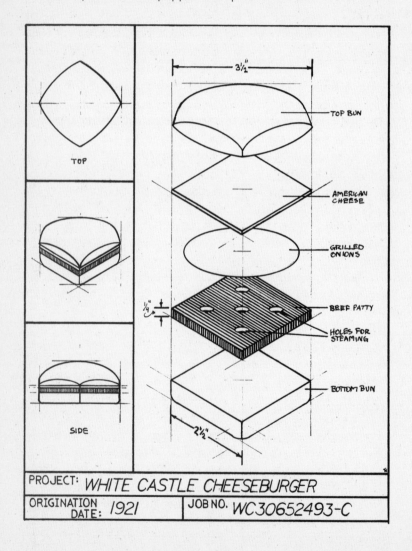

TOP

SIDE

3½"

TOP BUN

AMERICAN CHEESE

GRILLED ONIONS

¼"

BEEF PATTY

HOLES FOR STEAMING

BOTTOM BUN

2½"

PROJECT: WHITE CASTLE CHEESEBURGER

ORIGINATION DATE: 1921

JOB NO. WC30652493-C

6. On each pile of onions place a frozen beef patty. You may have to spread the onions out some so that the hamburger lies flat. Salt each patty as it cooks.
7. Cook each burger for 4 to 5 minutes on the onions. If you made the burgers thin enough, the holes will ensure that each patty is cooked thoroughly without flipping them over.
8. Assemble by sandwiching the patty and onions between each grilled bun.
- MAKES 16 BURGERS

TIDBITS

If you want to add pickle slices to your burger, as you can at White Castle outlets, stack them on top of the grilled onions.

For a cheeseburger, you'll have to cut a slice of American cheese to the same size as your burger, and then it goes on top of the onions, under the pickles, if you use pickles. Got it?

• • • •

YORK
PEPPERMINT
PATTIE

In York, Pennsylvania, Henry C. Kessler first concocted this confection in the late 1930s at his candy factory, the York Cone Company. The company was originally established to make ice cream cones, but by the end of World War II, the peppermint patty had become so popular that the company discontinued all other products. In 1972, the company was sold to Peter Paul, manufacturers of Almond Joy and Mounds. Cadbury USA purchased the firm in 1978, and in 1988 the York Peppermint Pattie became the property of Hershey USA.

Many chocolate-covered peppermints had been made before the York Peppermint Pattie came on the market, but Kessler's version was firm and crisp, while the competition was soft and gummy. One former employee and York resident remembered the final test the patty went through before it left the factory. "It was a snap test. If the candy didn't break clean in the middle, it was a second."

For years, seconds were sold to visitors at the plant for fifty cents a pound.

1 egg white	Cornstarch for dusting
4 cups powdered sugar	One 12-ounce bag semisweet
1/3 cup light corn syrup	chocolate chips
1/2 teaspoon peppermint oil or extract	

1. In a medium bowl, beat the egg white until frothy but not stiff. Don't use a plastic bowl for this.

2. Slowly add the powdered sugar while blending with an electric mixer set on medium speed.
3. Add the corn syrup and peppermint oil or extract and knead the mixture with your hands until it has the smooth consistency of dough. Add more powdered sugar if necessary, until mixture is no longer sticky.

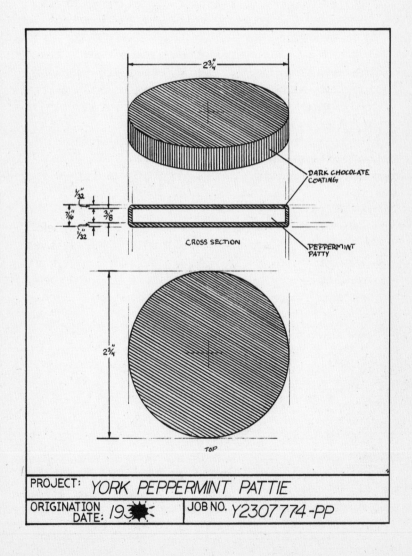

2¾"

DARK CHOCOLATE
COATING

¹⁄₃₂"
⁷⁄₁₆" ³⁄₈"
¹⁄₃₂"

CROSS SECTION

PEPPERMINT
PATTY

2¾"

TOP

PROJECT: YORK PEPPERMINT PATTIE

ORIGINATION
DATE: 193█   JOB NO. Y2307774-PP

4. Using a surface and rolling pin heavily dusted with cornstarch, roll out the peppermint dough until it is about ¼ inch thick.
5. Punch out circles of peppermint dough with a biscuit cutter or a clean can with a diameter of about 2½ inches. Make approximately 20, place them on plates or cookie sheets, and let them firm up in the refrigerator, about 45 minutes.
6. Melt the chocolate chips in a microwave set on high for 2 minutes. Stir halfway through the heating time. Melt thoroughly, but do not overheat.
7. Drop each patty into the chocolate and coat completely. Using a large serving fork, or 2 dinner forks, one in each hand, lift the coated patty from the chocolate. Gently tap the forks against the bowl to knock off the excess chocolate, and place each patty on wax paper.
8. Chill the peppermint patties until firm, about 30 minutes.

· MAKES 20 PEPPERMINT PATTIES

• • • •

T R A D E M A R K S

"A&W Root Beer" is a registered trademark of A&W Beverages, Inc.

"Arby's" is a registered trademark of Arby's, Inc.

"Bailey's" and "Original Irish Cream" are registered trademarks of R&A Bailey & Co.

"Carl's Jr.," "Santa Fe Chicken," "Western Bacon Cheeseburger," "Junior Western Bacon Cheeseburger," and "Double Western Bacon Cheeseburger" are registered trademarks of Carl Karcher Enterprises.

"Cinnabon" is a registered trademark of Cinnabon World Famous Cinnamon Rolls.

"Dunkin' Donuts" is a registered trademark of Dunkin' Donuts, Inc.

"El Pollo Loco" is a registered trademark of Flagstar Corporation.

"Heath" and "Bits o' Brickle" are registered trademarks of L. S. Heath & Sons, Inc.

"Keebler," "Pecan Sandies," and "Toffee Sandies" are registered trademarks of Keebler Company.

"Little Caesar's," "Crazy Bread," and "Crazy Sauce" are registered trademarks of Little Caesar's Enterprises, Inc.

"M&M/Mars," "Mars," "Mars Almond Bar," "Milky Way," and "3 Musketeers" are registered trademarks of Mars, Inc.

"McDonald's," "Filet-O-Fish," and "Quarter Pounder" are registered trademarks of McDonald's Corporation.

"Nabisco," "Chips Ahoy!" "Nutter Butter," "Oreo," "Double Stuf," and "Big Stuf" are registered trademarks of Nabisco Brands, Inc.

"Nestlé," "Crunch," and "100 Grand Bar" are registered trademarks of Nestlé USA, Inc.

"Popeye's Famous Fried Chicken" and "Popeye's Chicken & Biscuits" are registered trademarks of America's Favorite Chicken Company, Inc.

"Snapple" is a registered trademark of Snapple Beverage Corporation.

"Stark," "Necco," and "Mary Jane" are registered trademarks of Necco Candy Co.

"Strawberry Julius" and "Pineapple Julius" are registered trademarks of International Dairy Queen, Inc.

"J&J" and "Super Pretzel" are registered trademarks of J&J Snack Foods Corporation.

"Taco Bell" is a registered trademark of PepsiCo.

"Tastykake" is a registered trademark of Tasty Baking Company.

"Wendy's" and "Wendy's Single" are registered trademarks of Wendy's International.

"White Castle" is a registered trademark of White Castle System, Inc.

"York" is a registered trademark of Hershey Foods Corporation.

INDEX

℗ **Plume**

GREAT RECIPE COLLECTIONS

☐ **TOTAL JUICING** *Over 125 Healthful and Delicious Ways to Use Fresh Fruit and Vegetable Juices* **by Elaine LaLanne with Richard Benyo.** Provides up-to-date, accurate information and more than 125 recipes for great juice combinations and for fruit and vegetable pulp. (269288—$10.00)

☐ **BETTER BY MICROWAVE by Lori Longbotham and Marie Simmons.** Packed with tantalizing recipes, this comprehensive cookbook and guide provides helpful tips on microwave safety, accessories, and special uses for the microwave plus complete preparation and cooking times and important nutritional information.
(269857—$12.00)

☐ **TOP SECRET RECIPES** *Creating Kitchen Clones of America's Favorite Brand-Name Foods* **by Todd Wilbur.** This irresistible collection of cloned recipes is perfect— whether you're a kid or just a kid at heart, you'll have a great time making the incredible clones of a McDonald's BigMac, a Burger King Whopper, Tastykake Butterscotch Krimpets, a YooHoo Chocolate Drink and much more! (269954—$10.00)

☐ **MORE TOP SECRET RECIPES** *More Fabulous Kitchen Clones of America's Favorite Brand-Name Foods.* **by Todd Wilbur.** Now, you can make home versions of over 50 *more* of your favorite foods. All of them are shockingly easy to prepare— with ingredients from your local supermarket! These fabulous clones leave out the preservatives and include suggestions for making high-cholesterol dishes lower in fat—without changing the tastes we all love. (272998—$9.95)

Prices slightly higher in Canada.

Visa and Mastercard holders can order Plume, Meridian, and Dutton books by calling **1-800-253-6476**.
They are also available at your local bookstore. Allow 4-6 weeks for delivery.
This offer is subject to change without notice.